The Story of Nethy Bridge

The Story of Nethy Bridge:
A Highland Village

By
Jane Macaulay

Librario

Published by
Librario Publishing Ltd.

ISBN : 978-1-909238-05-3

Copies can be ordered from retail
or via the internet at :

www.librario.com

or from :

Brough House
Milton Brodie
Kinloss
Morayshire
IV36 2UA

Tel : 01343 850178

Cover design and layout by
Kings Design Studio, India

Printed and bound in Great Britain

© Jane Macaulay 2013

The Author has asserted her moral right to be
identified as the Author of this Work. No part of this book
may be reproduced, stored in a retrieval system, or transmitted
by any means, electronic, mechanical, photocopying, recording,
or otherwise, without permission from the author.

Acknowledgements

With special thanks to former County Councillor Alistair McCook for his memories and photos, to historians Dr Jean Munro and George Dixon, to Sandy McCook for helping to process the photographs, and to much of the population of Nethy Bridge, whose brains I have been shamelessly picking for the past two years, especially:

Rita and Bill Templeton, The Rev Jim and Aileen MacEwen, Donnie Black Snr, Edie Robertson, Jimmy MacLeod, Ian Kennedy, Barbara Millar, Alec Morley, Bette Calder, Mona Cameron, Elizabeth Fleming, Stuart Black, Howard Edge, Lorimer Gray, Neil Sutherland, Sandy McCook, Richard and Pat Eccles, Robert Wiles-Gill, Ross Watson, Malcolm and Deirdre McCreath, Michael Mustard, Barbara Murray, Andy Young ... and many more

Also, former Nethy residents:

Celia Smart, Elgin; Catriona MacArthur, Inverness; Robbie Smith, Nairn; Frank Macaulay and Grace Smith, Grantown-on-Spey,

and memories of conversations with my late Father, John Macaulay, and Grandfather William Grant Macaulay

Bibliography

T.M. Devine: *The Scottish Nation, 1700-2000*, Penguin, 2000

The Rev W Forsyth: *In the Shadow of Cairngorm*, The Northern Counties Publishing Company Ltd, Inverness, 1900 (reprinted Bothan Publications, 1999)

Sir Thomas Dick Lauder: *Highland Rambles and Long Legends to Shorten the Way*, Adam and Charles Black, 1853

Sir Thomas Dick Lauder: *The Great Moray Floods of 1829*, 1832, Reprinted Librario Publishing Ltd

IF Grant: *Highland Folk Ways*, Routledge and Kegan Paul Ltd, 1961 Reprinted Birlinn Ltd, 1995

Elizabeth Grant of Rothiemurchus: *Memoirs of a Highland Lady*, John Murray, 1898

Reprinted Canongate Classics, 1988

ARB Haldane: *The Drove Roads of Scotland*, Birlinn, 2008

Emma Wood: *The Hydro Boys*, Luath Press Ltd, 2002

Elspeth Grant: *Abernethy Forest, Its People and Its Past*, The Arkleton Trust, 1994

A.S. Grant: *The Games. Its Characters*. Highland Printers, Inverness, 1999

A.S. Grant: *Abernethy Golf Club Centenary, 1893-1993*, Highland Printers, Inverness, 1993

J.M. Mathieson: *Place Names of Strathspey: Abernethy and Kincardine*, for the Gaelic Society of Inverness, 1952

Dr Jean Munro: *The Church in Abernethy*, 2000 (unpublished)

Unpublished writings by A.S. Grant, Nethy Bridge, and William Macaulay, Australia
Statistical Accounts of the United Parishes of Abernethy and Kinchardine: 1791-99, the Rev John Grant; 1834-45, the Rev Donald Martin
Statistical Account for the Parish of Cromdale, 1834-45, the Rev James Grant
Highland Archive Centre, Inverness: Censuses for 1841, 1861, 1871, 1881, 1891;
Abernethy and Kincardine School Board Minutes, 1873-1918
Minutes of Strathspey Farmers' Club, 1846-1991
The Nethy newsletter, all editions, 2005-2012

Websites:
www.nethybridge.com/history
www.ambaile.org.uk
www.churchofscotland.org.uk
www.abernethy.org.uk
www.clangrant.org
www.dorback.com
www.heatherlea.com
www.oldkirknethybridge.org
www.cairngorms.co.uk

Introduction

'*N*ever let the facts stand in the way of a good story' is a quote attributed to Mark Twain and repeated many times with regard to modern journalism. The sentiment could go back much further in history, since much of what we think of as fact was originally passed down by word of mouth. Long before the Internet, and even before books were in common use, recalling the past was the job of the story-teller, who was quite well aware that most people would rather hear a good story than the recounting of dry facts.

In writing this book, I have tried hard to uncover the facts, while keeping aware that much of what has come down from the past may very well be embroidered or stretched to make a good story. There were story-tellers within my own family and many of the things I learned as a child were later discovered to be suspect, yet there was always a grain of truth there too, worth recording and passing on.

At the same time, as I began to write down the information, I found that it naturally worked itself into a story, moving relentlessly forward from the days of the hunter-gatherers to crofters taming a few acres on which to grow their crops, tend their animals and raise their families. I traced the changes in land ownership and the development of viable industries of forestry and farming; the creation of a central village around the bridge and the train station, the advent of tourism, winter sports and conservation, the immigration of people from other parts of the country. It is a story with progress and reversals, conflicts and reconciliations and a cast of lively characters.

This is not meant to be an exhaustive historical account of the area – more a picture of how our village came to be, how it changed and developed,

The Story of Nethy Bridge

particularly during the busy years of the 19th and 20th centuries, and how it is developing still, as we race forward into the 21st. Change has been so rapid, and so many people have moved in and out of the area, that there is a danger of much of our heritage being forgotten, so I have tried to capture as much as possible before it is too late.

This is the place where I grew up, as did four previous generations of my family, and for that reason I make no apologies for my deep affection for the village. I know I am not alone, however, in seeing Nethy Bridge as somewhere very special, poised between mountains, forests, rivers and lochs, a place where it is possible to achieve a very special sense of peace, beauty and harmony.

Chapter 1

Early Days: Cottars, Caterans and an ancient Castle

Throughout the centuries, this little corner of the world has meant many things to many different people. For farmers, it is an oasis of fertile ground in the midst of barren mountain country; for wildlife enthusiasts, it is a place on the edge of the forest, ideal for the observation of birds, beasts and plants. Some of the older inhabitants sigh for the days when it was a bustling village with a selection of shops and two railway stations. Younger ones are excited about the possibilities for outdoor sports, while others are simply here for the marvellous views of mountain and moorland, river and loch. For me, born and brought up here and returning now later in life, it is a place to call home, a place where peace and quiet, beauty and wildlife are all available. But there is also a sense of community, where people still help each other out and take the time to stop and chat, stepping outside the frantic treadmill of 21st century life.

The actual village of Nethy Bridge is not particularly old, having evolved gradually after the building of the Telford-designed bridge in 1810. The parish of Abernethy, on the other hand, is much older, dating at least as far back as around 1200, when a charter was granted by Richard, Bishop of Moray to Patrick, son of William, to set up a church here. Abernethy, centred on the old church on the Grantown road was linked with Kincardine, centred on the church on the Rothiemurchus road. Between them, they formed a parish which stretched along the east bank of the Spey; from Balmenach and the edge of the Cromdale Hills in the north as far as the foot of Cairngorm to the south and Brig o' Broon to the west. Included within its boundaries were the districts of Dorback and Tulloch and gradually there arose a number of small settlements such as Garlyne, Causer, Lynstock and Duack-side. The building of substantial stone bridges in the late 18th and early 19th centuries created new settlements – Old Bridge of Nethy, otherwise known as Old Bridge End and Bridge of Nethy, known as Nethy Bridge, the latter being the name by which, eventually the whole area came to be known.

Although indisputably part of the Highlands, Abernethy is less remote than much of the region. Early travellers, who tended to come to Scotland by sea, could approach the area from the Moray Firth, travelling up the valley of the Spey. The river and its tributaries also provided much fertile land so that survival here was less harsh than in other areas.

The name Abernethy is a bit of an enigma. 'Aber', which is found in place names throughout the British Isles, means the place where a smaller river joins a larger one (in this case the Nethy flowing into the Spey) but as for the word 'Nethy', its origin and meaning are lost somewhere in the past. It may come from the Gaelic 'An fheith-fhiadhaich', meaning a wild, turbulent river – those who have seen it in flood will relate to this – or from 'An Eitighich', meaning 'gullet', suggesting that the water passes through a gorge. Alternatively, it may go back earlier, to Pictish times and might even be connected with Nechtan, the Pictish king. Equally likely is that it comes from the Celtic word 'Nedd', meaning 'gleaming' – which is how it can appear on a lovely sunny day.

Little is known about the very early history but the area was probably populated by Picts. A ruin above Delbog in Tulloch may have been one of their burial places and Pictish arrow heads have been found on the gravelly banks of the Nethy. The most ancient building in Abernethy is Castle Roy which stands on what is now the old road to Grantown beside the old church. In a map from the 1580s it appears as 'Abernethy Castle', but later maps call it Castle Roy, although no one seems to know the origin of the name, which means 'red'. It was probably built more as a fortress than a castle with stone outer walls to protect the people in times of attack and wooden structures within the walls, of which no traces remain. It is sometimes claimed to be the oldest castle in Scotland and this may be because, while there are many older fortifications throughout the Highlands, these tend to be round and are known as brochs. Castle Roy on the other hand, is square in shape in common with other Norman buildings. While positive information about the castle is limited, there are many myths and legends, including that of a tunnel beneath the Spey, maybe even as far as Muckrach Castle on the other side of Dulnain Bridge. If this were true it would be an amazing feat of engineering: sadly, no trace of any tunnel has ever been found and neither has the treasure which is supposed to be buried there. Ghosts are also supposed to have been seen around the time of the summer solstice.

Like the rest of Scotland, all the land around Abernethy was owned by nobles who had been appointed by the kings. The first recorded owners were the Comyns (or Cummings), a Norman family who are supposed to have been responsible for building Castle Roy. When Robert the Bruce became king, however, the Comyns fell out of favour as they had fought against him, with Bruce famously killing the Red Comyn in Dumfries in 1306, so their land was confiscated. A charter of 1384 notes that the 'lands of Abernethy' were among those granted by King Robert to his son Alexander, Earl of Buchan, who was later to become known as the Wolf of Badenoch. From his strongholds at the castles of Lochindorb, Loch an Eilean and Ruthven Castle, he carried out a campaign of destruction which culminated in his burning of Elgin Cathedral in 1390, following a long-term dispute with the Bishop of Moray.

By the 15th century, 'the lands and lordship of Abernethy' were in the hands of the chiefs of Clan Grant, who paid a rent of £40 to the Earl of Moray. The Earl finally lost his power over the area, although it is said that he held on to a tiny piece of land Torran Mhoid (the Mote Hill), a little to the east of Castle Roy, so that he could still be called the Lord of Abernethy. Meanwhile, in the mid -16th century, many of the tenants began to show their loyalty to their clan leader by taking the surname Grant – a name which is still the most common in Nethy Bridge today. In the 18th century, the Grants were to become even more powerful as landlords when Ludovic Grant of Grant married a daughter of the Earl of Seafield, whose lands stretched along the Morayshire coast. Succeeding landowners held both the titles Grant of Grant and Earl of Seafield until, in the 20th century, the lack of a male heir meant that the titles were split, with the land being retained by the Seafields, while the chieftainship of Clan Grant passed to another branch of the family

The main home of the lairds of Grant was Freuchie, later becoming known as Castle Grant, beside the present-day town of Grantown-on-Spey. From 1566 to 1582 the laird's eldest son Duncan Grant made his home at Coulnakyle, the principal farm in Abernethy on the fertile plain beside the Spey. So much was he considered part of the parish that he was nicknamed 'Duncan of Abernethy' or 'Duncan of the Woods'. After his death, Coulnakyle continued to be considered as the laird's summer seat – a sort of earlier-day holiday home. Perhaps because of this connection with the clan chiefs, Coulnakyle played a role in various historical events. General Montrose took shelter there briefly in 1644 while his Royalist forces were being pursued by those of the Duke of Argyll. His men apparently, were able to hide in the Forest of Abernethy, which at that point stretched as far as the farm. ('Coulnakyle' in Gaelic means 'Back of the Woods')'. In 1689, General McKay stopped there while escaping from the forces of 'Bonnie' Dundee who was leading a rebellion against William of Orange, the Protestant king of the time. McKay was impressed by Coulnakyle, which he described as 'a summer dwelling of Grant's where there were some meadows and fields of corn proper for the nature of the party whose strength was most in horse'. Dundee was killed at the Battle of Killiecrankie but the Jacobite forces, now led by General Buchan, moved to Coulnakyle and used it as a staging point for the Battle of Cromdale – sung about in *The Haughs of Cromdale*. The song used to be performed by Scottish folk group the Corries who, for some reason, insisting on softening the word to 'haws' instead of pronouncing the guttural Scottish 'ch' sound at the end of 'haughs – which is the local name for the Cromdale Hills and for its village pub.

Otherwise, the main farms were rented out to kinsmen of the Grant chief, known as tacksmen, who sub-let parcels of land to tenants or cottars, each of whom held a few arable strips on which to grow their crops and shared a further piece of rougher land as common grazing.

As landlords go, the Grants appear to have been reasonable, with a genuine concern for their tenants who they saw as a kind of extended family. However, it was accepted practice that all the game on their estate was there for their exclusive use. The tenants tended to see things differently and there is supposed to be an old Gaelic saying that everyone is entitled to 'a deer from the forest and a fish from the river'. Poaching, therefore, was always considered an accepted part of the way of life – although not one that was condoned by the laird's factors and keepers. One particularly famous poacher was William Smith of Rhinuigh, a croft well up in the Tulloch hills, who roamed the hills shooting red deer at his leisure and also wrote some fine Gaelic poetry, including 'At the Burn of Lochan Uaine', subtitled 'The Poacher's Dream'. Poaching families have continued to exist through the generations, with skills being passed down from father to son.

Clearly the best land in Abernethy was closest to the Spey, so the farms alongside it – Coulnakyle, Rothiemoon, Balliemore, Balliefirth and Auchernack – appear regularly in ancient documents, albeit in a variety of different spellings! The names were originally Gaelic, or possibly date even further back to the mysterious Pictish language, but were written down by English speakers, hence the apparent randomness of the spellings. Balliefirth (or Balliefurth) was an important crossing place of the Spey in the days before bridges, as it was where the Grants crossed to Ballintomb, the meeting place of the clan. Balliemore (the Big Place) was for many years the home of the estate factor, a person who wielded much power amongst the residents, as is shown in the frequently quoted 'Crofter's Prayer':

"From the floods of the Nethy, from the storms of the Geal Charn and the wrath of the factor, Good Lord deliver us."

Other names which appear as far back as there were written records are mainly places along the banks of the smaller rivers or burns, places like Craigmore and Garlyne on the Aultmore; Ellaneorn and Lettoch on the Dorback, and Culvoulin, later to be renamed Birchfield, on the Duack. 'Culvoulin' means 'behind the mill' – suggesting that there was a mill on the Duack well before the one recorded as being built in the 1860s, so it is fitting that Explore Abernethy has chosen to site its reconstructed mill lade here.

Lurg was also important in the 17th century as the home of Robert Grant, chamberlain to one of the Grant lairds, who praised him for his 'great care and diligence in holding courts and purging the country of knaverie and pyckeries.' A portrait of Robert Grant of Lurg, an imposing man with a great bushy beard, used to hang in Castle Grant.

Apart from the ubiquitous 'Grant', other surnames familiar in Abernethy go back a long way and have interesting stories behind them. The name Cameron is common, some of them particularly tall people. This is supposed to be because they are descended from twelve of the biggest, strongest young men in Lochaber, who came here with a daughter of Lochiel, chief of clan Cameron, who married a Grant of Kincardine in the early 16th century. Apparently the lady was afraid for her life in the wild country of Strathspey and insisted on bringing them with her as bodyguards. The Stewart (or Stuart) family, according to legend, are descended from two brothers from Atholl, who escaped over the hills after a clan dispute with some Robertsons. One of them is supposed to have settled on the farm of Laintachan, subsequently marrying the farmer's daughter. The Black family consider themselves to be descendants of the Stuarts, who changed their names after Culloden to avoid persecution, and many retain 'Stuart' as a middle name.

For the earliest inhabitants, the hunters and gatherers, Abernethy was a good place to live off the land, catching trout and salmon from the rivers and deer from the forests, as well as gathering the native fruits. Blaeberries grew in the woods, averons (otherwise known as cloudberries) in the mountains and the open moorland was home to 'braolach', or cowberries (a small, sharp relative of the American cranberry). These were particularly prolific after the forest had been cleared, either by forest fire – an occurrence which seems to have been quite common from earliest times, often as a result of clan warfare – or by deliberate felling of the trees in an attempt to rid the land of wolves.

Gradually, the people became farmers or cottars, living in clusters of turf and heather-thatched cottages in the more fertile areas, growing strips of oats and bere (a grain similar to barley and suited to upland areas) with some kale (a form of cabbage) and grazing a few sheep, goats and the all-important black cattle. These were not the large, beefy Aberdeen-Angus so common here today, but an early form of Highland cattle – horned, long-coated and hardy enough to live outside most of the year. The sheep, on the other hand, were small, delicate beasts of an early breed no longer in existence and they had to be sheltered at night in 'sheep-cotes'. In a 1770s map, 'sheep-cotes' are marked in the moor behind Lettoch. Goats were also kept and allowed to graze on the hills. Craiggowrie, the hill beside Tulloch, means 'the hill of the goats' and Meall a Bhuachaille, at the other end of the Tulloch Hills, means 'the herds' hill' – not 'shepherd's hill' as it is sometimes translated – suggesting that all the various domestic animals were herded there in the summer. The names of crofts well up the Nethy – Rynuie,

Rynettin and Rynerrich, for example – contain 'Ruigh', the Gaelic word for shieling. It suggests that the larger farms operated the shieling system, with the animals being moved up to the hills throughout the summer months, along with some people to keep an eye on them. Remains of such buildings have also been found high up in the Cairngorms.

The grain that was grown on the small, rough plots was not sufficient to nourish the people throughout the year, so they used the milk from their animals to make various forms of cheese, selling off the surplus beasts to cattle drovers who walked them through the hills to the trysts at Crieff or Falkirk, or further south into England. The money which they received would pay the cottars' rents, with some left over to buy essentials such as salt. They rarely ate meat, but would sometimes take blood from the living cattle and eat it, mixed with oats, as a primitive form of black pudding. Subsistence became slightly easier when potatoes were introduced in the 17th century, as it was possible to produce more from the small plots, but this proved a mixed blessing when blight affected the crop in the 19th century, causing terrible hardship for those who had relied too heavily on this vegetable.

Their dwellings were heated by a fire in the middle of the floor, the smoke meandering around the living area before escaping through a hole in the thatch. This burned peat, the remains of ancient forests preserved in the many peat bogs around the area.

As in many primitive societies, cattle were seen as a source of wealth: the richer and more influential a person, the more cattle he owned. It is not surprising, then, that cattle theft was one of the commonest of crimes, one which has also gained a cloak of romance as we look back at it through the years. In the hills behind Abernethy is the Thieves' Pass, a section of a track leading from Lochaber and the wild lands of the west to the fertile, cattle-rich plains along the Moray Firth coast. Within the parish of Abernethy, the pass comes from Glenmore by the Green Loch and Revoan, in front of Carn a Beadhair (pronounced 'Carn Vyower') then along the back of Carn Cnuic (prounced 'Carn Frooach') and Carn a Loinne, coming out at

Dorback Lodge where it splits in two. One pass takes it towards Brig o' Broon on the Tomintoul road and onwards towards Morayshire; the other further up the Dorback and over the mountains to Aberdeenshire. Along these tracks the cattle-thieves (or 'caterans') would travel under cover of darkness, collecting herds of well fed cattle and driving them back to the west. Unfortunately, they were not averse to picking up a few Abernethy cattle along the way and there is a famous letter from Cameron of Lochiel to James Grant of Freuchie, written in 1645, apologising because his men had taken some Grant cattle, whereas it was common knowledge that cattle from the Laigh of Moray were fair game 'to Morayland, quhair all men taks their prey'.

A tragedy occurred on the Thieves' Pass at the croft known as the Feith (pronounced Fay), now a lunch hut on the Dorback estate. A Cameron man was shot by a certain Alan Grant of Tulloch, who was stationed there, employed to protect the cattle against the caterans. Different versions of the story suggest that the Camerons were there to avenge an earlier killing of one of their clan or even that there was a woman involved. The tradition however, is that there is still a stone there, in a field called Straan Cameronich (field of the Camerons), which bears a blood stain that has never faded.

Justice was meted out by the Church or by the Baron Bailies, hereditary officials appointed by the lairds. Every Sunday, offenders were named and shamed in front of the congregation for offences such as adultery, Sabbath-breaking (such as cutting timber on a Sunday), defamation (or slandering someone's character) or behaving inappropriately at funerals (for example 'violing, dancing and such-like heathenish enormities'). The Kirk Session could impose fines for the less serious offences and the money thus raised was often used for useful purposes such as building bridges across the Dorback and the Nethy. More serious offences would be referred to the Baron Bailies who met at various places including Rothiemoon, Coulnakyle and possibly Balliemore, which has a pond beside it supposed to have been used for the drowning of witches. These Baron Bailies had powers to banish people from the parish, as in the case of a number of young women in 1748 who were guilty not just of adultery but of 'giving up fathers to their children that cannot answer the charge laid against them'.

A common penalty for theft was to nail the offender by one ear to a post, to force them to stand there for an hour and then to 'break the grip nailed without drawing of the nail'. A particularly barbaric punishment was given to Margaret Bain of Inchtomach, a croft high up the Nethy, who was found guilty of 'haunting with the Halkit Stirk' (or hanging out with a notorious cattle thief of the time). She was to be stripped to the waist, scourged by the hangman with thirty stripes, have both her ears cut off and then be banished from Strathspey for ever.

For those who were considered inveterate thieves, the punishment might well have been hanging which would have been carried out at the Gallows tree, just across the road from the present-day Lynstock Crescent. This impressive Scots pine could still be seen until its remains were cut down in the 1970s and it is said that bones have been dug up just along the road, opposite the old Smithy, which was supposed to have been where the bodies were buried. Another hanging place was at Tomachrochar, a farm on the Boat of Garten road where the present-day sheepdog trials are held. The Gaelic name means 'Hangman's Hill'.

From early times, the Church was absolutely central to society. Recorded history seems to start with the coming of Christianity, and there are supposed to have been chapels at Congash on the road to Cromdale, Lainchoil in Dorback and at the appropriately named Chapelton in Tulloch. The old Abernethy church, beside the stronghold of Castle Roy, is first recorded on a map in 1580, but it seems likely that there was a Catholic church on the site considerably earlier, before the Reformation that brought about the Church of Scotland, which held its first General Assembly in 1560. As John Knox thundered against Mary Queen of Scots and the evils of 'popery and idolatry', he was particularly concerned about the North of Scotland, sending a Commissioner to Moray 'because it is complained that the North country for the most part is destitute of ministers'. The commissioner reported back that there was very little they could do because the inhabitants all spoke 'Irish' (Gaelic) and begged that someone would be found who could converse in that language. For the next few decades complaints continued about the state of churches in the north, but Abernethy did indeed embrace the Church of Scotland, unlike some of the less accessible parts of the Highlands, which have retained a Catholic church until today. The parish was part of the Bishopric of Moray which was ruled from Elgin Cathedral, built in 1224 and known as 'the Lantern of the North', presumably because it spread the light of Christianity throughout the North of Scotland. Traditionally, Abernethy was part of Moray, ruled from Elgin, while Kincardine belonged to Inverness shire. Later both became part of The Highland Region.

The first recorded minister of Abernethy Church is William Farquharson in 1580 and he was followed by Patrick Grant in 1585, Colin Mackenzie in 1633, Roderick Mackenzie in 1642, John Sanderson in 1656 and Colin Nicholson in 1670. The old language problem remained, however, for there was a complaint by the Synod of Moray in 1656 that Abernethy was one of twelve parishes in their jurisdiction where the people had no English and the minister had no Gaelic.

The next minister, James Grant, was to fall foul of the political climate of the time. As a Jacobite, he refused to acknowledge the new king, William of Orange, from the pulpit and was subsequently removed from his charge, leaving Abernethy without a permanent minister for around twenty years, until the arrival of William Grant in 1709.

The Church of Abernethy is dedicated to St George, although he is supposed to be a replacement for some forgotten Celtic saint, and Abernethy traditionally held an annual George Fair, first in the church grounds, later at Balnagowan.

The Church was also responsible for education in the area, after John Knox had insisted that schools should be provided in each parish, particularly for the education of poor country children. In Abernethy, the first mention of setting up a school comes in the form of a petition to Parliament in 1658 from the Presbytery of Strathspey to allow money for the erection of schools in the parishes of Abernethy and Rothiemurchus. The result of this petition is not known but it is believed that a school was first erected in the church yard, and a later one at Croft Croy, which was then part of the Church lands but is now part of Abernethy Golf Course.

Money to pay for the building of the school and the payment of the teachers was provided from fines imposed on wrong-doers. However, an Act passed in 1696 forced the landowner or 'heritor', to provide accommodation and a salary for teachers who were chosen by the landowner and the Church. Those who could afford it paid for their children's education, but poor children who were recommended were educated free.

The history of these early days is somewhat sketchy, but a picture is beginning to emerge of a settled community living off the land, with the Church as a focal point, education for many of their children and a strict sense of justice. They are unlikely to have moved far from their hamlets or crofts or had much contact with the politics of the outside world, As that world gradually became industrialised, Abernethy was to play a major part, particularly when it came to supplying what the area had to offer: timber from the forests and beef from the fertile river plains.

Chapter 2

1700–1810: Forestry, Farming and the Good Sir James

The signs on the approaches to Nethy Bridge tell us that this is 'the Forest Village'. This is a fairly recent attempt at branding, but there is no question that the trees around us have played a very big part in the development of our community.

The Abernethy Forest, which laps the village and stretches up to the lower slopes of the Cairngorms, is part of the original Caledonian Forest. While the sections closest to the village have been cleared and replanted several times, some of the more remote stretches have been left relatively untouched for thousands of years.

The early landowners saw the forest chiefly as an area for sport, a place where they could take their guests to shoot deer, in fact everything that ran or flew about the forest and the mountains was considered fair game. Capercaillie and ptarmigan were particularly prized, in fact considered fit for a king, and in 1617 a letter from the Privy Council to the Laird of Grant requested that some of these birds be sent to Newcastle for King James, who was travelling north to Scotland for the first time since taking over the throne of Great Britain. More than 200 years later, in 1822, King George IV made his famous visit to Edinburgh, coming ashore at Leith and donning his very own version of full Highland dress. Once again, Highland game played its part, as is described in Elizabeth Grant's *Memoirs of a Highland Lady*, in which she explains how her father sent from Rothiemurchus 'fifty brace of ptarmigan, all shot by one man in one day', along with some bottles of 'pure Glenlivet whiskey' to Holyrood House in Edinburgh to welcome the king – a present which stood him in good stead since he was rewarded with a post as judge in India.

The forest was also seen as a supply of timber for building purposes and trees were felled on a relatively small scale but it was not until the early 18th century that forestry in Abernethy really took off. There was a great demand for wood at the time as a building material in the cities, which were springing up further south and, more particularly, for the mighty wooden ships which were engaged in business around the world. The fact that so many wars were being fought throughout this century also increased the demand for timber.

In 1704 William Batt, foreman to Her Majesty's Mast Maker in Deptford, compiled a report on the suitability of Scottish pines for ships' masts, in which he singled out those from the Abernethy Forest as 'likeliest to serve her Majesty and Government'. A later report also recommended the forest as a great source of 'tar, pitch, rosin and other naval supplies'.

Transporting tall pine trees from the depths of the Abernethy Forest to the London docks may sound like a difficult enterprise, but Abernethy was fortunate in having several small burns running through the forest. These burns were dammed far up and the trees were dragged to the dams using horses. When enough water had accumulated, the sluices were opened so that the volume of water propelled the trees downwards and into the Spey.

There were six dams in the forest, the remains of which can be seen in some places: Duack Dam, south-east of Tore Hill; Garrochar Dam (now Loch a Gharbh Choire), by Ryvoan; Big Dam, south-east of Rynettin; Cromault Dam, at the confluence of three burns, south of Carn Cnuic; Faesheallach Dam (now Loch na Spiorad), near Lurg, and Funalt Dam, just above Nethy Bridge, with an outlet flowing into the Duack. When the logs reached the Spey, they were sorted and stamped with the owner's initials, then floated down to the mouth of the river, there to be loaded on to ships or, at a later date, used in the ship-building works which developed there, at Garmouth on the Moray Firth. Not all the timber reached the Spey, however, as some would be selected on its way downstream for the use of sawmills nearer home. Dr William Forsyth (writer of *In the Shadow of Cairngorm*), was a boy at the Dell of Abernethy in the early 19th century, and he remembers the sawmiller there, Benjamin Lobban, pulling out trees as they floated down the Nethy.

The logs were originally floated down the Spey either individually or tied loosely together and were accompanied by a man in a currach – a wicker basket covered with ox hide. Later the method was improved by building the logs into rafts held together by iron loops. Two men travelled on each raft with 'cleeks' – wooden poles with a two-pointed iron head – to manoeuvre the rafts. According to Dr Forsyth, the men, the 'floaters', were able to make the journey in twelve hours, setting out early in the morning and walking back as far as Rothes to spend the night before returning the rest of the way the following day. The rafts also proved a useful mode of transport, ferrying people and produce up and down the river.

The most significant timber project in the area came in 1728, when Sir James the landlord of the time, agreed to sell 60,000 fir trees to the York Buildings Company, which also leased the buildings and fields of Coulnakyle as a centre for their operations. This company had originally been set up in 1691 to supply water to the fashionable parts of London.

Later, it diversified into buying up estates in the Scottish Highlands which had been confiscated from lairds who took part in the 1715 Jacobite rebellion. The Abernethy Forest was recommended to the company by one Aaron Hill, a London poet, who also wrote and produced plays and was manager of the famous Drury Lane Theatre. So impressed was he by the forest, which he visited in 1726, that he wrote a poem to his wife about 'The Golden Groves of Abernethy'. Their operations were on a massive scale, erecting temporary wooden houses for accommodation, as well as a number of sawmills, and employing 120 horses and all manner of machinery.

As well as supplying timber for ship-building, they used the branches to make another popular fuel of the time, charcoal. Some of this was exported as far as Holland and some was used to smelt iron ore which had been excavated at the Lecht, to the south of Tomintoul, and transported to Abernethy by ponies. There were at least two iron works beside the Nethy, one at Coulnakyle and one which may have been near Aldersyde, just down river from the Black Bridge. Sir Thomas Dick Lauder, in his book *The Moray Floods*, claimed that the beams and framework of the higher mill were revealed by the 'Muckle Spate' of 1829, one hundred years after it was in use. Traces of what may have been the mill can still be seen, but otherwise the only evidence that it ever existed is in some remaining pieces of iron said to be worked there, including a 10 foot long iron pillar used until the 1960s to hold up part of the byre at Dell Farm.

There is also a possibility that the ironworks was at Balnagowan, as the original part of the house was built at this time and the name means 'place of the smiths', suggesting that iron 'smiths' were based there. Certainly, Balnagowan was associated with the sawmill at the bottom of the brae, which may also date from about this time.

Unfortunately, the company had over-extended itself and left Abernethy in 1737, having run up enormous debts. According to the

Rev John Grant, writer of the Abernethy section of the 1790s *Statistical Account of Scotland*:

> "They were the most profuse and profligate set that ever were heard of then in this corner ... their extravagancies of every kind ruined themselves and corrupted others ... They used to display their vanity by bon-fires, tar-barrels and opening hogsheads of brandy to the country people, by which five of them died in one night ...".

The timber trade continued to thrive, however, after the demise of the York Buildings Company. In the second half of the 18th century, Sir Ludovick Grant began to appoint foresters to look after the woods, in payment for which they received the tenancy of the farm of Rynettin, plus half the money received from fining people who were caught stealing wood. In 1765, an enquiry was received about providing wooden water pipes for the New River Company of London. The woods of Abernethy were considered particularly suitable and for this purpose a boring mill was built at Dell, to convert the tree trunks into pipes. It is not clear, however, whether any of these pipes were actually used in London. The River Nethy proved a great source of water power and as well as the boring mill, there were at least four sawmills built along its banks, most notably at Balnagowan, Coulnakyle, Lower Dell and, possibly, Ellaneorn. The Balnagowan mill, which was still in use until 1965, is remembered by the name Mill Lane, while the course of the original mill lade can still be traced at Lower Dell, circling an area known as 'the island' and remembered by the house name Island Bank. Similarly, the area inside the lade of the Coulnakyle mill, close to the present-day sewerage works, was still known as 'the island' in the 1960s when Spencer's sideshows used to be sited there every August. Other water-driven mills included several meal mills, the most significant one being the Mill of Garlyne on the Aultmore, which appears in 18th century maps. It was still being used up to World War II, with farmers bringing their oat crops to be turned into oatmeal. There was also a meal mill at Craigmore and for a short while in the mid-19th century, a carding mill on the Dorback, just up stream from Lettoch, where shepherds could take their fleeces to be prepared for spinning. There was also a 'clogging' mill near Forest Lodge, where wooden shoes were made.

More industry was sited at Backharn, beside the track that leads from Garlyne to the Grantown road, close to Auchernack. Here there was a slate quarry, producing thick, heavy slates which were used on some of the older houses, gradually replacing heather thatch as a roofing material. Traces of this quarry could still be seen as recently as the 1960s.

For the Highlands of Scotland in general, the most significant event of the 18th century was the 1745 Jacobite Rebellion. Bonnie Prince Charlie landed at Moidart on the West Coast, gathered an army consisting mainly of Highland clans and marched south, defeating the Government Army to take control of Edinburgh. They continued South through England but were disappointed in their hopes of rallying more to their cause. They were also hopeful that a French army was about to come to their aid but this too failed to materialise. Meanwhile the Government army, which had initially been taken by surprise, had time to recall troops who had been fighting on the Continent. Faced with much greater numbers, the Jacobite army was forced to retreat to Inverness where they were soundly defeated on Drumossie Moor at the Battle of Culloden. With the aim of suppressing the wild Highlanders once and for all, the English troops, led by the Prince William Duke of Cumberland – or 'Butcher' Cumberland to the Jacobites – remained in the area, carrying out atrocities among the poor families while searching for the Prince and his followers. Eventually, with the help of Flora Macdonald, the Prince succeeded in escaping to France, via the Isle of Skye. It is said that the Duke of Cumberland is remembered in the name of two very different flowers: 'Sweet William' by the English and 'Stinking Willie', the local name for the weed, ragwort, by the Scots.

Many romantic notions have grown up around this event, not least the belief that the rebellion was all about Scottish Highlanders versus English. This was not really the case, as the causes of the Rebellion were complicated and there were Scots and English on both sides. Not all the clans chose to follow the Prince, the Grants of Strathspey being a case in point (although other septs of the Grant clan did fight on the Jacobite side). The laird of the time, James, received an appeal from Prince Charlie in August 1745, but the letter was returned unopened to the Secretary of State. As a result, Abernethy was not much affected by the fall-out from Culloden.

The area's only real claim to involvement is that one high-ranking Jacobite, John Roy Stuart, is supposed to have hidden here for a time. As he had been born at the Knock, Kincardine, he went into hiding in the area. He moved around Badenoch and Strathspey and at one point he is supposed to have spent a night at Balnagowan and danced with the guests at a wedding which was taking place there. He went from there to Badnedin, where the cave in which he is supposed to have hidden can still be seen. However, he had to flee, dressed as an old beggar, when he heard that the redcoats were approaching. He then moved to Connage, on the other side of the hill from Badnedin, but left there to join up with the Prince, who was hiding at Ben Alder in Badenoch. He later accompanied him to France where he died in 1752, without ever returning to Scotland.

There is also a local belief that the ghosts of Jacobite soldiers returning from Culloden have been seen at Castle Roy and though there is no evidence that any such soldiers were ever there, it is possible that some may have passed that way en route to Ruthven Barracks at Kingussie, where a number of the forces regrouped after the battle.

The years after Culloden took a dreadful toll throughout the Highlands, as the old system of clan chiefs who were caring landlords began to disintegrate. Even those chiefs who had not been involved in the Rebellion were in many cases finding themselves deeply in debt and they took harsh measures to make money out of their Highland estates, demanding higher rents or forcing their people from the land. This was not the case in Abernethy, however. The chiefs of Grant had been successful businessmen and throughout the 18th and 19th centuries, worked hard to improve their estates without too much upheaval for the population. 'Improving' was the watchword of the 18th century all over Britain. One good result of Culloden was that the presence of Hanoverian soldiers in the new military forts at Fort William, Fort Augustus and Fort George helped to bring to an end the lawlessness of the caterans. Whenever a robbery was reported, detachments of men were sent out to round up the perpetrators, who were duly hanged at Inverness. Although it may have marked the end of a colourful era, it did make it easier for the inhabitants to prosper in business contact with the outside world.

The population of the country was increasing, many people were moving into the cities in the south and Britain was involved with various wars in continental Europe. Consequently there was a great need for produce such as beef and wool.

Beef was already being supplied by the black cattle. Dealers from the south moved around the area, bargaining with the farmers and crofters over the price of calves or older cattle, which were then walked south by drovers who followed the old routes through the hills – the Lairig Ghru (the Gloomy Pass) which those who have walked it will know is strewn with boulders, or the Lairig an Laoigh (Pass of the Calves), which was considered gentler for the young animals' feet. Other drovers' routes were through Glenfeshie and Glen Geldie or through Glen Tromie over the Minigeig Pass into Glenbruar, where they could join with the main routes south – just as the tour buses all pause now at the House of Bruar, disgorging their flocks of travellers to shop or graze there! From here they would proceed to the market at Crieff and then onwards through England, often still accompanied by their Scottish drovers. A drover's path through the hills of Yorkshire still boasts the remains of a church known as the 'Scots chapel' where, presumably, the drovers stopped to worship. When they reached their destinations in the south, it is said that the drovers sometimes stayed a while, for social or business reasons, but sent their collie dogs to find their own way home. These clever animals would follow the route taken by their masters and would be fed by the same people who had entertained them on their way south.

The scraggy little Highland sheep, however, were not much good for supplying the wool required in the emerging cities. Consequently a new breed, the Blackface, was introduced into Abernethy from the Borders. This breed was hardier and more able to thrive in harsh conditions and was considered more suitable than the larger Cheviot, being introduced to the North and West Highlands. Unlike the infamous landlords of the Clearances, who removed their tenants to make way for the sheep and their Borders shepherds, the Grants introduced the new sheep onto established farms with existing tenants. They believed, apparently, that it was good to keep a high population on the land so that many men could be 'raised for the regiment' in time of war.

In the Statistical Account, the Rev John Grant describes something of the effect of these new sheep on the farms of the time:

> "By the tenants increasing their number of sheep, and still striving to keep up their former number of black cattle, neither the sheep can be expected to be sold fat nor the cattle in general in decent marketable condition, by which means they must always be sold at prices inferior to what they would fetch if properly grazed."

The problem, as he saw it, was that there was not enough pasture for them in the summer and not enough straw to feed them through the winter. It was to be a few more years before the introduction of the turnip was to revolutionise animal husbandry by providing a more nutritious winter feed.

The main agricultural improvement of the 18th century was the addition of lime to the soil, which counteracted the acidity and thus enabled people to grow greater quantities of hay and grain crops. In time, lime kilns were to be erected on every plot of land, but by the 1790s, according to the

Rev Grant, they had only been introduced to five farms in the parish – he does not name them.

The writer of this account, 'Parson John', was popular throughout the parish where he was minister for 60 years, succeeding William Grant, who had held the post for an almost as impressive 51 years. Parson John, who is remembered by a plaque in the old Abernethy Church, is described by Elizabeth Grant in her *Memoirs of a Highland Lady,* as her favourite of the ministers who used to visit them in Rothiemurchus:

> "He was a little, merry man, fond of good eating, very fond of good drinking, no great hand at a sermon, but a capital hand at either the filling or the emptying of a bowl of punch".

Elizabeth Grant also describes how he liked to give an account from the pulpit of the latest news of the time, in those days the progress of the wars against Napoleon. On one occasion he had given them a particularly exciting version of events, before discovering that the newspaper account from which he had taken them had not been totally accurate. The following week he was forced to backtrack, beginning his service by declaiming from the pulpit: "My brethren, it was a' lies I told you last Sabbath day".

According to William Forsyth's *In the Shadow of Cairngorm,* Parson John was very concerned to hear that some of his parishioners had been stealing potatoes during the 1780s when there was much famine throughout the area as a result of severe weather; so he announced from the pulpit that he had a good stock of potatoes at Croftcroy and he would prefer it if people asked him for them than took them unasked.

This was in stark contrast to his successor Donald Martin who, during a later period of poor harvest, castigated his parishioners from the pulpit, telling them it was their fault for being sinful. One bold member of the congregation approached him after the service to point out that he must be as sinful as any of them, since the crops at Croftcroy were just as poor as theirs.

Education, though neither free nor compulsory, had a strong presence in the area. Lachlan Shaw, the first recorded schoolmaster in Abernethy, was later to be ordained as a minister and to go on to write an important *History of Moray*. The Scottish Society for the Promotion of Christian Knowledge (SSPCK) provided funds for the provision of schools in remote areas, sometimes called charity or adventure schools, and there is evidence that these existed at some time at Muckrach in Dorback, at Lurg, in Tulloch and in Kincardine. In 1750 a new schoolhouse was being built for Abernethy, with 'defaulters' (people convicted of a crime) being instructed to bring timber and set up couples for the roof of the building. Just where the school was sited at this stage is, however, uncertain.

As the 18th century progressed, the Grant chiefs continued to improve their lands. Sir Ludovick, who had been responsible for employing foresters, encouraged his tenant farmers to plant potatoes and turnips and spread lime. He also attempted to 'improve' the morals of his tenants by reducing the number of ale houses, stating that he thought seven or eight were quite enough for the whole of Strathspey, claiming that: "They are generally the Pest of the Tenants' morals. In them they spend their time and money, make quarrels and idle bargains and occasion great dissolution and vice of every kind." This was a cause taken up by a succession of Grant lairds, but we can only speculate how successful they were in the long term.

The landlord who made the greatest impression on the area was Ludovick's son, 'The Good Sir James', who took over the estate in 1764. He is supposed to have earned the name because, in 1799 when poor weather had caused the harvest to fail, he sold his Edinburgh townhouse and borrowed 1000 pounds from a wealthy clansman on business in London (Sir Robert Grant, whose son was later to found Charlestown of Aberlour in Lower Speyside) to buy grain and potatoes for his starving tenants. His greatest achievement was to found the new town of Grantown-on-Spey in 1765 as a centre for weaving, but he also did many things to improve other parts of the estate. At Castle Grant he set up a training school for stonemasons, who were going to be much used for building works.

One of his grand schemes was to change the course of the River Nethy, cutting out many of its twists and turns and building bulwarks to force the water into a straighter course, thus increasing the arable acreage as well as making it easier for timber floating. Thus he created the shape of the Nethy more-or-less as we know it today, with the gentle loop where the Riverside path now runs from the Black Bridge to the main Nethy Bridge, and another straight stretch below the bridge and towards Coulnakyle. At the same time, in 1771, a single-arched stone bridge, 17 feet wide and with a span of 45 feet, was planned and built across the Nethy, about 100 metres upriver from the present-day bridge, carrying the road across from Balnagowan to Culvardie. History does not relate whether there were earlier, wooden bridges there or at another site, although there certainly must have been recognised fords. Bridges, apparently, had a short life span owing to the regular violent floods, and even this sturdy-looking stone bridge was not to last long, being swept away somewhere around the turn of the century. Today no trace of it remains and only the plan and map, drawn up in Castle Grant, show us that it ever existed. The name 'Old Bridge End' was used for many years to describe the area round about and is still the name of one of the houses in Culvardie.

A number of impressive new houses were also built around this time, most notably the main house at Coulnakyle, designed by the famous architect John Adam, who had been brought to the area to design some alterations to Castle Grant. Adam may also have been involved in designing the main house at Birchfield, which is said to have been occupied by the family of one of the younger sons of the chief of clan Grant. The plaster cornicing of the ceilings appears to be of French design and similar to that of Castle Grant.

A new church was built, on the same site as the older one, after many years of complaints that it was in a poor state of repair or that it did not have sufficient seating for all the people who wanted to attend. In 1748, people were being asked 'to provide and carry to the churchyard heather and other materials necessary for compleating the reparation of the kirk' – proving that it was still a thatched building at that time.

In 1762, however, the church was inspected by a gathering of representatives of the Presbytery, the session and some wrights and masons, who decided it was no longer worth repairing and that a new church should be built. The Good Sir James wanted it to be built 'on the muir above Culnakyle', but he does not appear to have got his way as the new, slate-roofed church, built by Alexander Cuie from Keith, was on the same site as the original one.

The original manse, on the other side of the road from the church, is now the main building of the Christian-run outdoor centre known as the Abernethy Trust. The first recorded manse had been built in 1624, but this was replaced by a much grander building in 1769, designed by architect John Scott.

So the Improvements of the 18th century went a long way towards shaping the Abernethy area we know today, but there was still no central village. The first step towards its creation was taken in the early years of the 19th century and was one of the last great achievements of the Good Sir James. Having raised the funds for numerous roads throughout his estates, he was anxious to improve the route through Abernethy and to build a new bridge across the river to replace the one which had been swept away. The Government of the time had commissioned the great Scottish engineer Thomas Telford to carry out a grand scheme to improve communications in the North of Scotland, so Sir James turned to the commissioners for help. They agreed to meet 50% of the cost, which left Sir James to raise the other half. In order to help him with this, subscription lists were circulated in the area, under the supervision of schoolmaster William Macdonald.

Telford himself visited the site on June 2, 1809, and by the end of that month had drawn up plans for a completely new stretch of road from Abernethy Church to Mondhuie, including a single-arched bridge across the

Aultmore, close to the church.(This came to be known as the Bridge of Clark, although no one seems to know the origin of the name). He also designed a bridge across the Duack at the other end of the village, as well as a culvert across a small burn on what is now the village golf course. The most significant part of the plan, however, was for a three-arched bridge across the Nethy itself, some distance downstream of the 1770s bridge. A Kingussie mason, John Eason, was in charge of the first season's work, under the supervision of Telford's inspector, John Mitchell.

Preparation of the sites began before the end of August, 1809, but Mitchell advised Sir James that, with the approach of winter, the principal bridge should not be carried beyond the springs of the arches until the following year's building season. The construction of the arches, therefore, was under the charge of Moray man Thomas Urquhart, who had replaced Eason. Some of the masons involved in the work had to be brought from as far as Perth, but most of the labour, skilled as well as unskilled, was local.

By November 1810, the road and the four bridges were complete. Sir James only just lived to see his project to completion, as he died three months later. The road and bridges are still in use today and form the centre of the village that we now know as Nethy Bridge. It was to take another 50 years, however, and the introduction of a whole new form of transport, before the village began to take the shape that is familiar today.

Chapter 3

1810–1863: Sporting Tourists and the Start of a Village

The construction of the Telford-designed road and bridge may have marked a step forward in the development of Nethy Bridge, but the area was still isolated from the outside world. For travellers from any direction, it was still a long, difficult journey, over rough roads by coach or on horseback, so only the most intrepid traveller would venture here. The route from the south, over the Drumochter Pass, had been constructed nearly a century earlier, under the instructions of General Wade. The General's intention had been to bring order to the wild Highlands after the Jacobite rebellion of 1715 and to prevent another uprising, but it is said that the road worked to the disadvantage of the Government when it enabled Bonnie Prince Charlie's forces to move more quickly throughout the Highlands.

Elizabeth Grant, in her *Memoirs of a Highland Lady*, describes her family's long, tedious journey, by horse and carriage in the early years of the 19th century, from their winter home in the South of England to their summer residence at Rothiemurchus. The stretch from Edinburgh took three days and then there was the difficulty of crossing the Spey from Aviemore, by ford or ferry, long before there was a bridge there. She also describes the vast improvement in mail deliveries in 1813 when a stage coach began to travel, three times a week, over the hill from Perth to Inverness, dropping off packages of mail along the way. Previously, their mail had come by way of Aberdeen and Inverness, from where it was taken by a 'runner' to Grantown and another 'runner' to Rothiemurchus, taking many days in the process.

In earlier years, the Highlands was seen as a barren country populated by savages – a myth which was perpetuated by the Jacobite risings – but gradually the perception changed as a Romantic age began to see beauty in nature and wilderness. This was much encouraged by the writings of Sir Walter Scott, whose poetry and novels described a wild and beautiful countryside, 'Land of the Mountain and the Flood'.

When the war against France made it difficult for wealthy young men to do the 'Grand Tour' of Europe, they opted for the 'Grand Tour' of Scotland instead. Robert Burns carried out a Highland tour in 1787 and spent half a day with Sir James at Castle Grant but the area does not appear to have inspired him to compose any poetry, apart from writing in his notes: 'Strathspey: rich and romantic'. Colonel Thomas Thornton came as close as Badenoch in 1783, before writing his book, *Sporting Tour in the Northern Part of England and Great Part of the Highlands of Scotland*, which is supposed to have started the idea of hunting, shooting and fishing holidays. Then in 1842 Queen Victoria visited and fell in love with the Highlands, leading to her purchase and re-building 10 years later of the shooting lodge at Balmoral on Deeside – just over the Grampians from Strathspey ... and the future of tourism in the Highlands was assured.

Hunting, shooting and fishing had always been popular pastimes for the laird and his guests, who would be given permission to shoot grouse on the moors, roe deer in the forests, red deer on the mountains and hares wherever they could be found. It was not until the 1820s, however, that it came to be seen as a good idea to rent out areas of land to 'sporting tourists', thus ensuring a good income for the landowner. The first of the Nethy Bridge residences to become a shooting lodge was probably Coulnakyle which, previously, was being farmed by a Captain James MacDonald. Among the early tenants was Englishman Richard Winsloe, who was so taken by the place that he made it a home for himself and his family from 1838 to 1846.

Dorback Lodge and Revack Lodge were built in the 1850s, while the whole of Abernethy Forest was rented out to wealthy shooting tenants, including Lord and Lady Stamford and Warrington. Initially they stayed at the former head forester's house at the Dell, which became Dell Lodge. It is believed that another lodge was built further up the Nethy, before the construction, in 1883, of Forest Lodge – an impressive wooden building, originally painted in striking black and white – on a site which had previously been called Lynmagilbert. It is said that almost all the wood for this building was supplied locally, by the Duack Sawmill, also known as 'the Crofter's Mill', which a Mr McDonald had built on his croft. Sadly, Lord Stamford and Warrington died soon after the lodge was completed and his widow gave up the shooting estate. In his memory she arranged for the erection of the drinking fountain which still stands on the river bank across from the Post Office. There is a story that, when the Lady went South at the end of the season, she left a substantial amount of money with instructions for a fountain of polished red granite with ornate carving. However, the workmen spent most of the money drinking in the Abernethy Inn, eventually building a fountain of much cheaper sandstone, with the simple inscription, 'Drink Hearty'.

The downside of the rise of sporting tourism was that the estate removed many crofters, on the expiry of their leases, from their homes within the Abernethy Forest. This was the closest Abernethy came to the 'Clearances' being perpetrated by landlords across the Highlands, but the landlord of the time did take care to find other crofts or farms for the evictees. Between 1830 and 1869, around 20 crofts were cleared, leaving empty homesteads with names such as Inchtomach, Rhynuie, Ryduach and Boggleshannoch. Local farmer and Councillor Stuart Black, whose grandfather was moved from a croft far up Nethy side to a farm at Brig o' Broon, had been told that "they never were bitter, as the places they were moved to were at least as good, if not better than, the places they were moved from." Others were less enthusiastic about being moved from the places where they had been born and brought up, but it appears that some went on to be successful elsewhere, including the family of Duncan McAndrew, evicted from Inchtomach, whose descendants became successful breeders of Blackface sheep in Perthshire.

Others, perhaps too elderly to continue with the crofting life, were housed in a new 'estate' known as the 'Street of Kincardine', close to the little white church which has always been used by the Tulloch community – as can be seen from the many family graves in its churchyard.

A high fence was built around this forest, to keep the deer from escaping, with gates on the roads through Tulloch and for this reason 'gate houses' were erected, which can still be seen.

As far as provision for tourists was concerned, Nethy Bridge still had a long way to go. An early guidebook, *Guide to the Highlands and Islands of Scotland*, written by the Anderson brothers in 1834, mentions Castle Roy and adds: 'One other mile leads to the bridge of Nethy where there is a miserable house of refreshment.' This early travellers' inn appears to have been on a site close to the existing Nethy Bridge Hotel – but the description is no reflection on the current provision!

With Culloden well in the past, the days of clan feuds were pretty much history. The warlike tendencies of the Highlanders had been diverted into the British Army, by creating patriotic regiments with names such as Cameron Highlanders, Highland Light Infantry, Seaforth Highlanders and Gordon Highlanders. Many Nethy men enlisted and gained high ranks in the service of the British Empire. The Grants in Abernethy, Duthil and Cromdale had one last clan rising, however, on 12th March 1820, when word reached them that the election of a Member of Parliament had caused a riot in Elgin and as a result, Lady Anne Grant was in danger of her life. Led by Captain Grant, Birchfield, and Mr Forsyth, head forester at the Dell, 150 men mustered at Nethy Bridge at 6p.m. on the Sunday and set out, armed only with sticks, on a march to Elgin. They arrived at dawn, after the Cromdale contingent and before the Duthil deputation, all causing great consternation to the citizens of Elgin, who thought they were about to be attacked by a crowd of wild Highlanders. Whatever the cause of the dispute, it seems to have been settled amicably and the men finally returned to Nethy Bridge, footsore and weary but otherwise unharmed.

The first half of the 19th century was not an easy time for Abernethy, with severe weather conditions including several droughts around the start of the century when the crops failed and grain had to be brought in to feed the inhabitants. They were followed by a series of floods, the most severe of which was the Great Flood of 1829, 'The Muckle Spate' which affected a large area of the North of Scotland, specifically the valleys of the Spey and Findhorn and their many tributaries. The flood is described very graphically by Sir Thomas Dick Lauder in his book *The Great Moray Floods of 1829,* but he does appear to have been a little like the tabloid journalist of his day and, although he clearly states: "Startling as many of the facts may appear, the reader may be assured of their unquestionable accuracy", this does not preclude a hint of sensationalism. It is true however that, after a very dry summer, the heavens suddenly opened on the evening of the August 2nd and it continued to pour for 42 hours. According to Mr Forsyth the woods manager, who was making his way home from Rothiemurchus to the Dell, the whole valley of the Spey from Kingussie to Grantown was one vast lake. Turning up Nethy side, he discovered that the road (present-day Dell Road) had been washed away, so that he had to abandon his horse and make his way on foot. He was terrified to find that his home with his family inside it (including his son, the future minister and writer Dr Forsyth) was completely surrounded by water. With the help of a ladder he managed to cross the torrent and reach his family who were all safe, although the floor was covered by one foot of water. Several buildings were completely swept away, including a house at Drum, far up Dorback side and apparently twelve feet above the river. Inhabited by fox-hunter Alexander Fraser, his wife and six children, they escaped to higher ground from which they were able to watch the destruction of their home and all their possessions. The place is now the site of a magnificent lodge built by the owner of Dorback shooting estate. Up Nethy side, the barn and cowhouse at Inchtomach were also carried away, as was much agricultural land. In the village itself, the house of tailor Alexander Mitchell was washed away and the water flooded the smithy, filling up the forge, as well as carrying away an entire wooden sawmill from somewhere upstream. The bridge, just nineteen years after its construction, suffered serious damage to one of its three arches, but this was later mended and it has remained whole until today. Lauder also claims that the flood caused a diversion in the course of the river, though it is unclear exactly how it was affected, since the main changes seem to have been deliberately created earlier by the Good Sir James. The flood, or Lauder's description of it, forms the subject of Landseer's huge, detailed, highly dramatic painting, *Flood in the Highlands,* on display in Aberdeen Art Gallery. It depicts a terrified family, wrapped in their plaids and surrounded by their beasts, sitting on top of their turf roof while the flood waters swirl around them – the type of romantic view of Highlanders so beloved of Queen Victoria's favourite artist.

Other serious floods were reported in 1846 and 1849, while in January 1861 the *Glasgow Herald* reported an ice flood from which it was fortunate that the bridge suffered no further damage: "On Monday morning, the village of Nethy Bridge ran the narrowest risk possible of being swept away by the ice. Just at dawn of day, the ice on the Nethy broke up suddenly, about a mile and a half above Nethy Bridge, came hurling down like a huge mountain, sweeping everything within its reach right before it, until arrested in its rapid career (but for a moment) by coming in contact with, and being dammed at, the bridge." The article goes on to describe the scene in the area which must be where the Community Centre and Post Office stand today: "The large square is filled with ice, the walls of the houses being excluded from view and creating the greatest consternation to the inmates."

There were also some horrendous snowstorms, including one on the Friday before Martinmas (at the end of November), 1826, when people had travelled from far around to the annual market at Tomintoul. As the storm blew up in the afternoon, most people remained in the village and waited for it to pass, but two people died – one of them Donald Cameron, who was making his way home to Culdunie in Abernethy but perished, along with his horse, at Lynbeg.

The potato blight of the 1840s, responsible for the dreadful famine in Ireland, also had its effect here but the result was less disastrous, since the people were less dependent on potatoes as a staple diet. Nevertheless there must have been much hardship in the area, with the farms and crofts struggling to support the population. In 1845, a change in the law altered the way the poor of the parish were looked after. Up to then, it had been the responsibility of the Church, who used the money from fining wrongdoers as well as collections at the church door, but now this duty was taken away from the Church and new Parochial Boards were set up, with members elected by rate-payers. Abernethy responded by building a number of 'lodging houses' – otherwise known as 'poor houses' – at the Causer, with eight being mentioned in the Census of 1861. Some of these buildings still remain, now known as Lynstock Cottages, behind Lynstock Crescent, as well as Causer Cottages beside the old smithy. The people who lived there were known as paupers or pensioners, and were often widows with no family to support them. They were supplied with basic necessities such as food and fuel.

Throughout all the hardship, education was still seen as a priority in the parish as it gave many young people a chance to escape from living at subsistence level. In the 1835 Statistical Account compiled by minister Donald Martin, it was reported that there were 'seldom fewer than

100 scholars', who were being taught Latin, English, arithmetic, book-keeping, English grammar, writing and mathematics. The report went on to say that, thanks to their education at Abernethy, there were 'many young men, now conducting business prosperously'. In 1837 a new school was built of stone, lime and slate, replacing the more basic structure of the previous century.

Many people moved out of the area altogether, either to the industrial cities which were springing up in the south or overseas to North America or Australia. It was part of a general migration at the time, which was particularly common among Scots. Schoolmaster William McDonald, who compiled the 1841 census notes:

"The population of the parish is 1832, being a decrease of the whole parish of 260 since the last census." He suggests that this has been brought about by severe weather conditions from 1835 to 1839 causing people to move to the towns and that this, "coupled with the number that emigrated to the colonies, may account for the decrease."

The demand for meat from the North of Scotland continued, however, and in Abernethy huge advances were being made in agriculture. In the Statistical Account, Donald Martin writes: "There are some farms with a high degree of improvement, having substantial and commodious buildings and fields properly cultivated by strong horses and implements of the best form."

It also says that lime is now in general use, even among 'the lower order of farmers (such as pay no more than six pounds of rent annually)', with the material being quarried nearby and burned in kilns on every farm, making good use of plentiful supplies of peat and dead wood.

The Statistical Account of the neighbouring parish of Cromdale has more to say about the state of agriculture and, since both parishes operated under the same landlords, it seems likely that circumstance were very similar. Here the compiler states that "the black cattle are chiefly of the West Highland breed and considered very superior. At the Highland Society's great cattle show in Inverness, the first premium was awarded to a tenant of this parish for the best Highland bull."

He goes on to praise the breed of horses, which has likewise been improved over the years, as well as the method of rotating crops, the building of fences and dry-stone dykes and the digging of ditches. Produce and animals, from Abernethy as well as Cromdale, were sold at four markets a year, as well as a number of cattle trysts, in the relatively new market town of Grantown.

In all this, says the account, "much credit is due to the Strathspey Farmers' Club, consisting of the gentlemen of the district." This club had originally been founded by the Good Sir James and it went from strength to strength throughout the century. The fact that its members consisted not only of farmers but also of bankers, merchants, ministers and doctors shows the importance of agriculture in the local economy.

In 1850, the club also looked into the possibility of supporting a veterinary surgeon in the area, as there was a great need for one. Mr W. Fraser, Bridge of Nethy, was anxious to study for such a qualification and the club considered supporting him, once they had ascertained how much help he would need. The records do not relate what came of this.

Inevitably, the Abernethy farmers most prominent in the society were initially those from the larger, Speyside farms of Rothiemoon, Tomachrochar, Coulnakyle, Balliemore, Balliefirth and Auchernack, but there was a notable win in the turnip section by Mr Kennedy, Dell.

Forestry was also flourishing, with 100 men being employed in the industry in 1839, each earning an annual wage of seven pounds. Wood was still being floated down the Spey from Broomhill to Garmouth, where there were now yards building ships from the timber. Not only were they cutting down trees but they were also cultivating their replacements and planting them out to provide for years to come. The nursery on Dell Road was established in 1855 by James Brown, then Estate Wood Manager, with the purpose of raising pine seedlings from seeds which the foresters collected in the Abernethy Forest. It was continued by John Grant Thompson in the 1860s and extended to thirteen acres in 1883. Ornamental trees such as Wellingtonia were planted there and paths, hedges and fences were laid out so that it was a pleasant place to walk. A kiln used to dry out the seeds for propagation has recently been transferred to Landmark Centre at Carrbridge. The nursery and the rest of the forest were looked after by a series of careful managers, including Mr Forsyth, father of the writer and, at a later date, Mr Stephen, who constructed a 'summer seat', a type of gazebo, using 112 different types of wood. A replica of this can now be seen at the back of the Abernethy Churchyard.

Balnagowan and Craigmore woods were planted at this time, as was the forest between Lettoch and the Dorback road. In a map of 1771 this area is described as 'dry moor ground ... a common pasture' but by the early 20th century the trees had grown up, ready to be cut down for the World War I war effort.

As people moved away from the cottar towns, a village was beginning to take shape, although not exactly where it is today. The greatest cluster of houses seems to have been in what is now Culvardie, at the end of the 1771 bridge, hence the area was known as 'Old Bridgend' or 'Old Bridge of Nethy'. Some of the oldest houses in the village can still be seen there although most have been rebuilt, modified by subsequent generations of people. In the census of 1841, two people there are listed as shoemakers and two as carpenters, one of them Lewis McCook, whose descendants still live there. 'Nethy Bridge' is also named in 1841 as the area around the new Telford bridge, but there are only three buildings there, one of them a blacksmith.

Walking up Dell Road from the bridge, there were no houses on the left until Straanmore, a two-acre croft owned by the Murray family. They grazed their animals in the field on the other side of the road, known for many years as 'Meggie Murray's Park'. A daughter, Margaret Murray, became the only remaining member to live there, into the early 20th century. Further up the road came the cluster of houses and the sawmill at the Dell (or Lower Dell, to distinguish it from Upper Dell up Dorback side) - the centre of the forestry industry. There was also Dell Farm, inhabited by the Kennedy family.

On the other side of the Nethy, Balnagowan was prominent at the top of the brae and then nothing more until the Causar, with a cluster of buildings including the blacksmith which operated until the 1960s. The building still survives, now a cottage appropriately named 'The Old Smithy'. Close by there is also an Iron Mill, inhabited by a cooper, a packer and a carrier. Further up are the farms of Lynstock, Ellaneorn, Lettoch, Clachaig and Lurg and various other small crofts.

Stretching out into the hills and forest along the Dorback and Tulloch roads, and as far as the edges of Grantown and Rothiemurchus, are scores of farms and crofts, homes not only to the tenant farmers and their families but also to countless farm workers, who made up the bulk of the population of the parish of Abernethy.

Soon afterwards, Dell Road was to be altered by the construction of what is now Nethy Bridge Church, originally the Free Church, which stands proudly at the top of the brae just above Culvardie. This was built in 1851 as the result of the Disruption of 1843 when the Free Church broke away from the Church of Scotland. In Abernethy, six of the Church elders 'came out' in favour of the establishment of the new church, but they had to wait six years before it could be built in their parish. One of the reasons for the Disruption was a dispute over the right of landlords to choose new ministers – the Free Church members believed that this should be done democratically, by the church members. As a result, many landowners refused to grant land on which the new, breakaway churches could be built. In Strathspey the process of granting the land was also delayed, but allegedly this was not because of the landlord, Earl Francis William, rather his elderly factor, Captain John Grant of Congash. He resisted all kinds of change and also happened to be a cousin of the current Nethy minister, James Stewart.

Apparently the Earl waited until his factor was dead before allowing the building to go ahead. The Free Church did not acquire a full-time minister until Walter Ross in 1862.

The two churches in the village were to become reunited in 1929, by which time the Church of Scotland had changed its method of appointing ministers. The church in Dell Road is still very recognisably designed to be a Free Church, being much starker and plainer than the old church (otherwise known as Abernethy Church, the East Church or the Old Kirk) beside Castle Roy. Being much more central to the village, however, it was the former Free Church which became the main church as the years went by.

By 1861, the village had grown slightly. There were now 13 houses at 'Old Nethy Bridge' and a Post Office at Duack Bridge. Up the road from the Free Church and its Manse were Seafield Cottages, housing three families (two of these houses remain and were, for years, inhabited by forestry workers). At the Causer there were nine houses in addition to eight 'poor lodgings', later to be increased in number.

It is easy to imagine Abernethy during the first 60 years of the 19th century as being a rather sleepy place, not much advanced from the previous century; slowly declining in population as it became more difficult to earn a living off the land, even though the Agricultural Revolution was making things more profitable for those who remained. All this was to be transformed however, by the one single event which changed the face of our village for ever: the coming of the railway!

Chapter 4

1863-1900: The Coming of the Railway and the Rise of Nethy Bridge

The inhabitants of Nethy Bridge have always had a love-hate relationship with tourism. Many of those who earn their livelihood from the traditional industries of farming and forestry have no wish to see their village turned into a kind of theme park or museum. However it is a fact that without the seasonal influx, Nethy Bridge would have been a very different place. The solid granite Victorian homes which line what is now called Dell Road give the village much of its character – we tend to think of them as traditional Nethy Bridge homes. Most were built by local inhabitants who had prospered in the second half of the 19th century, but their purpose was to let to summer visitors – prosperous families from Edinburgh, Dundee, Glasgow or further south. Most of these houses have a smaller cottage behind them, into which the local family could move while the visitors, complete with their staff of servants, rented the big house for a month or two in the summer. Winter tourists, of course, were a much later innovation.

What made all this possible was the coming of the railway in 1863. Access to the area may have improved slightly in the early years of the century, but it was still a long and arduous journey from the South by horse and carriage. The railway suddenly made it easy for visitors to come for holidays and for produce from the village to be transported to the south – in fact there is scarcely an aspect of life that was not totally transformed when trains began to steam into the two stations: Abernethy and Broomhill.

Abernethy Station was on the Strathspey line, a branch line of the Great North of Scotland Railway. The line ran alongside the Spey from the distillery area of Dufftown, through Craigellachie, Advie, Cromdale, and Grantown East Station (on the Nethy Bridge side of the Spey). The station buildings in Nethy Bridge are still there, used at the moment as hostel accommodation, and it is still possible to see the supports of the bridges which took it across the Nethy, just below the butcher's shop, and across the Spey, near Tomachrochar. The line then ran into Boat of Garten station on a track owned by Highland Railway and parallel to the track from Broomhill. At one time trains on both lines were timetabled to enter Boat of Garten junction station at much the same time and the drivers used to race to be the first into the station – terrifying passengers who did not realise they were on separate lines! Abernethy Station later changed its name to Nethy Bridge, supposedly because freight intended for our village kept ending up in Abernethy, Perthshire ... and vice versa!

Broomhill Station on the other side of the Spey (now the terminus of the revived Strathspey Steam Railway), was part of the Highland Railway and the original main route north to Inverness, via Grantown West Station (now part of an industrial estate) and across the Dava Moor to Forres. The direct route to Inverness, from Aviemore by Carr-Bridge and across the Slochd, was not built until 35 years later.

It is interesting to note that the arrival of the railway was not always seen in a positive light, perhaps much as the building of motorways was viewed in more recent times. Elizabeth Grant of Rothiemurchus, who had described the long, arduous journey north by horse and carriage from London to her family's Highland estate at the start of the 19th century, was less than complimentary about the later method of transport, which she describes as 'that thundering iron way'. Likewise, the Rev William Forsyth who, by coincidence, arrived in Nethy Bridge in the same year as the railway, quotes a poem by Professor (later Principal) Shairp of St Andrews University. '*A Cry from Craigellachie*', written in 1866, describes the relentless progress of the railway: 'Northward still the iron horses! Naught may stay their destined path'. Perhaps prophetically, the poem expresses concern that one result might be the disappearance of 'the ancient Gael' from the glens and their replacement by 'Saxon', 'Southron' and 'Cockney'!

Nevertheless, the railway was immediately perceived as a useful way to transport the area's produce farther afield, with an impressive wooden bridge being built across the Spey in 1863, specifically to transport timber from the Abernethy Forest to Broomhill Station. This early bridge was to be replaced in 1894 with the one which can still be seen today and has been described as 'the finest wooden bridge surviving in Scotland'.

The railway also brought changes to agriculture. Strathspey cattle, still required and much prized to feed the hungry people in the south, could now be transported much more efficiently by train while cattle dealers could also travel more easily into the area. Breeding lines improved, as farmers could travel further afield, to the sales at Perth, to buy bulls and rams and then have them transported home by train.

Coal was brought into the area changing the way people heated their houses. Now it was no longer necessary to cut peat or to gather firewood from the forest and it is notable that the houses built at this time have small fireplaces, suitable for coal rather than logs. The trains themselves used quantities of coal to power them and it is said that some of this somehow found its way to the side of the tracks where it was collected by locals for their own use.

People's diet became more varied, with fresh produce arriving daily on trains from the south and from the coast. A fish shop was opened, near to the Nethy station, selling fresh fish direct from Aberdeen.

House-building was also transformed, with the railway being used to transport materials into the area. Granite blocks, brought in from the quarries of Aberdeenshire, replaced the rougher local stone, which had generally been covered with an outer layer of the lime-based harling, as added protection from the elements. Smoother, finer slates arrived from the quarry at Ballachulish, near Fort William, replacing the heather thatch which was still prevalent on the older dwellings, or the thick, heavy slates from the nearby quarries of Backharn or Tomintoul.

The rise of Nethy Bridge after the opening of the railway can be seen very clearly from the Census returns of 1871, which show the central area around the bridge as greatly expanded from the four houses which were there ten years earlier. As though aware that this was the start of something significant, the compiler of the Census has drawn a line near the end, with the words: "End of village of Abernethy. Beginning of hamlet of Nethy Bridge." There follows a list of 13 houses, inhabited by such people as railway porter, railway guard, carriage inspector, railway labourer and a station agent. There are also two shoemakers, a merchant and a blacksmith. Also included in the 'hamlet' is the soon-to-be-defunct Female School, inhabited by schoolteacher Janet Fraser and a boarder, Henry McConnach, a dancing master from Logie-Coldstone, Aberdeenshire. The Abernethy Hotel is also listed (no longer an inn, the previous inn-keeper, Davie Burnett, having died as his widow is listed as living in Seafield Place), while the listings also include John McLeod, constable, indicating the start of a police presence in Nethy Bridge. The Post Office, however, is still at Duack Bridge.

At the same time, the village was extending up Dell Road. Culvardie, with three houses, is mentioned for the first time. The name means 'Back of the Meadow', which clearly refers to the present-day playing field, previously a part of the farm of Birchfield. In addition to four houses called Seafield Cottages, there are 10 called Seafield Place, stretching out along what is now known as Dell Road. There is also a notable increase in people from outside the parish, who have either moved here permanently or are passing through. The census-taker actually seems quite proud to report that staying as a guest at Duack Bridge was the Hon. Lewis Alexander Grant, son of the Earl of Seafield. Another home had as lodger a chartered surveyor from Ireland while, more prosaically, there was a hawker staying at one house and a pack merchant from Ireland at another – presumably come by train to sell their wares. The Free Church manse is inhabited by the Rev Keith from Alness and the Dell Sawmill is home to two sawmillers, an assistant forester and a woodcutter. At Dell Lodge we find a gamekeeper from England, while Lynmagilbert, later to become Forest Lodge, is home to Iain Grant, spinner and knitter.

Ten years later, in 1881, the most significant change is that some of these new houses have been given names, such as Bridge End House, (now the site of Tigh na Drochaid, Gaelic for House at the Bridge), Nethy Bridge House (now Nethy House) and Rose Cottage in Station Road, Birch Cottage in Dell Road and Woodside Cottage at Old Bridge End. Further up Dell Road is the grander Heather Brae Villa, built by William McDonald of Balnagowan, who had made his money as a wood merchant, dealing with the produce of his family's sawmill. Like so many new houses of the time, Heather Brae was built primarily for letting to summer visitors. An inventory taken after William's death in 1896 describes the villa as having: drawing room, dining room, smoking room, six bedrooms, two servants' bedrooms, a kitchen and a pantry, as well as very grand furnishings.

By 1891, the village has expanded some more, although it still seems to be quite spread out. Duack Bridge now boasts a shop, owned by William Methven who is described as a 'colporteur' – a seller of religious literature including Bibles. His wife Margaret runs the shop, along with a daughter

Maggie and a son Andrew who is described as an apprentice draper. Alex and Jane McKenzie live at Park Cottage, with Alex described as a mason and Jane as a merchant, and then there are two sister dressmakers, Jane and Maggie Blair.

In the centre of the present-day village, Nethy Bridge House is now a general merchant's, owned by David Smith; Rose Cottage is described as a boarding house, and Nethy Bridge Hotel is owned by James Grant and houses two barmaids, a cook and a waitress. There is a blacksmith beside the bridge, while on the other side of the river is Granite Cottage and the Volunteer Drill Hall. This latter was a wooden structure close to the bridge, where the bus shelter stands today. A large, rather uncomfortable wooden seat there marks the site today and makes use of some of the timber taken from it when it was demolished in the 1960s. The Drill Hall was primarily to keep young men in shape for the Army and was used for recruitment during World War I. The house of Caberfeidh (meaning 'stag's head', the regimental badge of the Seaforth Highlanders) was built beside it, to accommodate William Sinclair, drill sergeant.

The greatest expansion in 1891, however, is on Dell Road, with most of the grand granite houses we know of today – some of which have retained the same names, while others have now been changed. It is interesting to see that the original house names were English rather than Gaelic, probably because most of them were built with one aim in mind: to be let to summer visitors. Most of the inhabitants appear to have been bilingual at this stage, possibly speaking Gaelic at home but learning English at school, and they most probably saw English as the language of sophistication. The fashion for Gaelic house names, often called after mountains, was to come later – often, ironically, by incomers from the south.

So in 1891 we have Juniper, Fern, Willow and Greenwood Cottages at Duackside, while on Dell Road we have Diamond, Birch, Rosewood, Ivy, Hawthorn (now Morlich) and Clifton (now Torsithe) Cottages. Among them is the Gaelic-named Dalbuiack (place of the yellow daisies), built for

William Grant, otherwise known as 'Old Dellie', and given the same name as his farm, across the Spey in Duthil. This was sometimes spelt, as clearly it was pronounced, 'Delbuiack'. Old Dellie was allegedly a local character, brought up in Tombae (a now abandoned farm between Rothiemoon and Tomachrochar) and part of a dynasty which was to be responsible for farming Rothiemoon, Birchfield and Tomdhu. As a younger man, he had been a 'floater', one of the tough breed responsible for floating timber down the Spey to Garmouth.

Also new in the 1891 Census is the magnificent Badendossan Villa, built for John Macaulay, who had the bakery at the corner of Culvardie. The story goes that the Dowager Countess had decreed that all the new houses would be built lined up close to the road, but that, while the surveyors' pins were in the ground, John got up early one morning and moved them, so that the new villa would have room for a croquet lawn in front of it. The name 'Badendossan' is also a mystery. Family tradition has it that it means 'At the Edge of the Forest', but Gaelic speakers dispute this. John Macaulay was himself a Gaelic speaker and knew what he was doing, so there is a distinct possibility that he invented a name which tripped readily off the tongue and would be attractive to possible clients.

It is notable that (with the exception of Clifton, which probably existed earlier without the name) most of the houses built around this time are lined up with the road, whereas those built at an earlier date are more often gable end to the road. Early builders were more concerned about wind direction, the houses generally faced South-east, than road alignment. There are also the rather more prosaically named Nethy Brae Cottage (now Ingledene) and Nethy Bank Cottage (now Tigh na Monadh) and the rather more exotic Iona, close to the Black Bridge. Crowley Cottage was named after the member of the York Building Society who ran the iron mill and built a well beside the Nethy. Crowley Cottage later became Wyona and is now Achnagoichan.

The main effect of the arrival of the railway was the massive spread of tourism, and the tourists of the time were distinctly upmarket. In 1898 the

Nethy Bridge Hotel was rebuilt on a much grander scale, the new building forming the nucleus of what is there today. Run by Alexander McKenzie, it had come a long way from the 'miserable house of refreshment' described some 60 years earlier. It was rebuilt and intended for the gentry – the only people who could afford hotel holidays at the time – and in its heyday, allegedly, was to play host to celebrities such as Cary Grant, Mae West and Lauren Bacall, who came mainly for the salmon fishing in the Spey.

This new building did not come without its attendant problems, one of them being the supply of water. In 1895, the Inverness-shire sanitary report stated that notice had been served on the inhabitants at the 'Cousar' to provide a suitable supply of water for each house. Water at the time was being taken from the Nethy, it was claimed, and this was deemed to be too polluted. (Actually, the source was a spring close to the Nethy, above Dell Lodge, the marks of which can still be seen today). The report suggested an alternative supply, from 'the Garlin spring', which could be brought in at a cost of £250. The inhabitants were clearly in no hurry to remedy this because three years later it is reported that:

"The water supply in Nethy Bridge Special District was very scarce last summer, the houses on the higher levels only getting an intermittent supply. Several new houses are in course of erection, particularly a large hotel, for which there is practically no supply available at present."

It may be a relief to know that the spring at the Garlyne, a little further up the Aultmore from Mill of Garlyne, was finally pressed into service and continued to supply the village with wholesome drinking water until the 1960s, when a new supply for Strathspey was brought from Loch Einich in the Cairngorms.

The coming of the railway in 1863 also coincided with the arrival of a new minister to the village: the Rev. Dr William Forsyth. As well as becoming involved with every aspect of village life, he was to write the all-encompassing *In the Shadow of Cairngorm*, a history of the parish of Abernethy and Kincardine which, ever since, has been the authoritative source of information about the history of the area. Forsyth was a popular minister, being a 'local boy' as he had been brought up at the Dell – later called Dell Lodge, where his father was Manager of the Seafield Woods. He had attended Abernethy Primary and Grantown Grammar School, followed by Aberdeen University where he gained an MA at the frighteningly young age of 18. He then studied Divinity and was licensed to preach by the Presbytery of Forres in 1846. He was minister at Ardersier and Dornoch before returning to his home village, where he remained until his death in 1907.

Dr Forsyth was also much involved with education in the village, becoming chairman of the newly-formed School Board after the Education Act of 1872 made education compulsory for all children aged five to 13 (raised to 14 in 1883 and 15 in 1945). The Act also brought education under control of the state instead of the Church, although there was a stipulation that the Church would continue to be involved. In the case of Nethy Bridge, not only was the chairman of the School Board the Church of Scotland minister but, on the few occasions when he was absent from meetings, his replacement was Walter Ross, Free Church minister. Also on the first Board were Seafield Estate factor John Smith, farmer James Edward of Birchfield and Donald Grant, described as a 'writer' (apparently a type of lawyer) in Grantown – not to be confused, presumably, with the schoolmaster of the time, who was also a Donald Grant. At later dates in the 19th century, the Board was to be joined by Mr Grant of the Nethy Bridge Hotel, baker John Macaulay, farmers Mr Stuart of Balliemore and Francis Grant of Tombae and wood merchant William MacDonald of Heatherbrae.

According to the School Board records for 1873, in the Parish of Abernethy and Kincardine, out of a population of 1752 there were 320 children between the ages of five and thirteen, of which 140 were attending school. Their needs were served by the Abernethy Public School, a 'female infant' school in the house now known as Carlthorpe, close to the present-day golf course, a Free Church school in Tulloch and an 'Adventure School' in Dorback. By the provision of the new Act, it was necessary to provide schools that were accessible to all the children in the far-flung parish, so there was some discussion about how this might best be achieved. While the public school was not large enough to take in all the pupils, it was thought that the female school might be acquired by the Board and used for extra classrooms. In fact, although part of the building was let out as a family home, the 'Old Female School' was where most School Board meetings were held for the next 30 years. There is mention of a classroom there, though no suggestion of what it was used for. The public school was expanded by gradual degrees over the years and new teachers were taken on – in the first place unqualified 'pupil teachers'.

At Tulloch, it was decided that the Free Church school was inadequate, so a new building was erected by Nethy Bridge mason Peter Macaulay and a male teacher was advertised for. At Dorback, however, it was decided to convert an existing building at Toberaie and to advertise for a female teacher, at a lower salary. There were so few children at Congash and Glenbrown that it was decided to ask that they be included in the nearer schools of Cromdale and Kirkmichael respectively – though in later years schoolrooms were found for them in existing houses closer to their homes. A school was, in fact, built at Brig o Broon and attended well into the 20th century. The building, now a house, can still be seen on the right of the road just before the foot of the big hill, as you head towards Tomintoul.

The new provisions were not universally welcomed and over the years the chief business of the school board seemed to be to challenge 'defaulters' – that is, parents who failed to send their children to school. Clearly many of the children were needed to boost the family economy and their absences were regularly explained by the fact that they were 'in service' with farmers in the area. Their chief job was herding, a task traditionally carried out by small boys in the days before there were fences to keep cattle off the crops. In the case of the girls, they were often required to help at home when their mothers were ill. Very often the reason for the children not attending was simply that their parents could not afford clothes or shoes for them, in which case requests were made to the Parochial Board to help them with these essentials. Another request to the Parish Council (as the Parochial Board had now become) was for a footbridge across the Aultmore, to make school-going easier for children on the wrong side of that burn. At least one explanation sounded like a poor excuse: one boy had not attended because he had chilblains, so could not put on his boots!

Again and again complaints were made that there were far too many 'defaulters' and that they should be dealt with more harshly – yet the list grew longer instead of shorter. There was also a regular list of requests to allow particular children to leave school at 13 rather than 14 and these were usually granted on the grounds that the children were 'necessarily and beneficially employed'. On the other hand, there were those from very far-flung corners who wanted their children to be educated and asked the School Board to fund special arrangements. For example, a tutor was arranged for the children of a gamekeeper at Glenmore, as were lodgings in Grantown, at a cost of £4 a year, for the son of Simon Smith, farmer at Lynemore.

In 1876, George Sorrie became the schoolmaster at Abernethy and he was followed in 1881 by Andrew Steele, who was to make a mark on the community. Steele demanded repairs to his dwelling as it was in poor condition and, in 1884, it was decided that it would be more worthwhile to build a new school house. At the same time, a piece of arable land on the north side of the school, measuring 2 roods 18 poles, was acquired from the Estate 'in perpetuity'. Later, Mr Steele was also to demand improvements to his barn and byre, indicating that there was also a croft attached to the school – but the Board refused this, considering that it was his own responsibility. A soup kitchen was erected in 1886 allowing the pupils a hot meal and in 1887 a 'treat' was given on the occasion of Queen Victoria's Diamond Jubilee. What that was remains a mystery!

Supplying water for the schools was always problematic. A pump had been sunk in the grounds of the Abernethy School, but in 1888 there were complaints that 'animal germs' had been found in the water. There were two options: sinking a new well or becoming connected to the Nethy Bridge Special Water District, which might also involve laying a pipe as far as the new 'paupers' cottages' at the Causer. The former option was chosen, however, as the latter one was considered too expensive. Often the school had to be closed for several weeks at a time because of epidemics of such things as measles, influenza, or most commonly, scarlet fever.

Another reason for closing the Dorback School in 1899 was that the teacher, Miss Geddes, wished to leave in July to take a trip to America. This was permitted as long as she was back to re-open the school in October.

During this period parents were still required to pay for their children's education, though collecting the fees was not always easy, but in 1891 the Board made a unanimous decision to abolish all fees, thus creating free education for all. Two years later, the school was recognised as a centre for higher education, enabling pupils to sit their higher leaving certificate, and for this an additional classroom was added for the advanced pupils.

The Old Abernethy Church was also improved and extended in the early 1870s, following demands by Dr Forsyth for a larger church and a vestry – the manse, he argued, was nearly a mile away, so he needed somewhere to change into his vestments. The architect involved was Alexander Marshall Mackenzie, who was to go on to design numerous churches throughout the North of Scotland, as well as many of the best known buildings in Aberdeen, including Marischal College. Church services were also brought up to date with the introduction of music. Traditionally, only metrical psalms were sung, unaccompanied, with a precentor singing the first line and the congregation repeating it, but paraphrases were gradually included. In 1898 hymn books were introduced for the first time followed, in 1902, by the Abernethy Church's first organ.

Dr Forsyth also founded a *Young Men's Mutual Improvement Society* at which improving lectures were given on topics which included local and natural history. Perhaps at a time of much change, with an influx of new people into the village, he felt the need to ensure that young people did not forget their own culture. A Reading Room was also established – the forerunner of today's Community Centre. The Mutual Improvement Society was to continue until the end of World War II, although it is good to know that by then it was also including young women.

In Nethy Bridge as elsewhere throughout Strathspey, the landowners were still very much revered at this time. There were great celebrations when the young Seafield heir, Ian Charles, celebrated his 21st birthday in 1872 and all tenants were invited to a party at Castle Grant with a marquee erected in the grounds. Equally, there was tremendous sadness when his father Sir John Charles, Earl of Seafield, died in 1881 and even more when the popular Ian Charles died suddenly just three years later – to be commemorated in name by the Ian Charles Hospital in Grantown. Since he had not married and left no direct heir, the estate was now in the control of his mother the Dowager Countess Lady Caroline and it is her name on the foot of all the leases that were issued during the grand spate of building which was to follow. Lady Caroline took a great personal interest in all of this and the stipulations in the leases, particularly that forbidding alcohol to be served, were her decision. This was to cause problems in years to come, with buildings such as the Community Centre and Golf Club unable to obtain a licence for many years.

With all the visitors in the village for the summer season, some entertainment was required, so the Abernethy Highland Games was held for the first time in 1880, at the beginning of September, the height of the shooting season, in a field at Coulnakyle. The competitions included feats of strength and speed which had traditionally been contested by young warrior clansmen, including: putting the heavy and light stones; throwing the heavy and light hammers; running high leap; hop, step and leap; vaulting with the pole; sack race; 300 yards race; two miles race, and boys' race. Tossing the caber was to be introduced later. There was also Highland dancing, including the Highland Fling and Gille Chaluim (later to become known as the Sword Dance). Both of these were supposed to have originated from war dances, but in fact had been developed in the post-Culloden years by Highland societies in Edinburgh and London.

Bagpipe playing was also included, but at the first Games there was only one competition, involving three competitors – a far cry from the numerous classes and massed pipe bands of today's Nethy Games. There was also a very popular contest, in the early Games, for 'Best-Dressed Highlander, at his own expense, home-made tartans preferred'. Unlike today, all the competitors, including the dancers, were male. One particularly famous name appears on the prize list for the heavy events: Donald Dinnie, who apparently threw the heavy hammer 96 feet.

Perhaps it was the success of the Highland Games which sparked the enthusiasm for Highland dancing in the village or perhaps, as Elizabeth Grant suggests in her *'Memoirs of a Highland Lady'*, the tradition had always been a popular one among Highlanders, passed from parents to children. Two local men, Lewie Geddes and Andrew Murray (both of whom still have descendants in Nethy Bridge), started a dancing school in the steading of the Geddes croft, Ellaneorn, half way up the Lettoch road. There a generation of Nethy young people were taught the skills of dances such as the Highland fling, the sword dance and the Seann Truibhas ('unwanted trousers') which is supposed to mimic the motions of Highlanders shaking off the hated trousers which they had been forced to wear in lieu of the kilt after the defeat at Culloden. It is said that the two Nethy men even went to Paris, so show off their dancing skills at the Great Exhibition of 1900.

The Games continued to be held at Coulnakyle until the outbreak of World War I when they were discontinued, to be revived after World War II at their present site behind the village hall.

The Abernethy Golf Club was opened in 1893, for the recreation of both visitors and locals. The first course was laid out at Balliemore and was opened with much pomp by Sir Hendry McAndrew, one of a group of 30 who had travelled from Inverness for the occasion. It was declared to be 'eminently suitable for the game and should prove to be one of the finest in the North'. Unfortunately, this was not the case as the land, so close to the River Spey, produced a rich crop of grass which was not easy to keep in check in the days before mechanical lawnmowers. There was also a complaint that it was too far to walk from the village and the station. So, two years later, the minister (Dr Forsyth) was asked if he was prepared to give up his right to the church croft of Croftcroy. He readily agreed and a lease was drawn up with the Seafield Estate. A committee was formed, with Dr Forsyth as president, head forester J.L. Stephen as vice-president and Andrew Steele, local schoolmaster, as captain, in which post he remained until his retirement in 1921.

Serious crime has never been prevalent in Nethy Bridge, with one shocking exception – the murder of police Constable King in Tulloch in December 1898. The story goes that a certain Allan McCallum, who had spent some time as a shepherd in the Falkland Islands and was believed to have been suffering from depression, was living in Tulloch. He was summoned to appear at court in Inverness on a charge of poaching, but he failed to turn up and was fined in his absence. Constable King and the Boat of Garten policeman Constable McNiven were sent to get him to sign an interdict but, on seeing them approach, McCallum ran out with his gun. The two policemen hunted for him all day and were about to give up when word reached them that he had been seen re-entering his house. As they approached it this time, McCallum appeared with his gun and shot Constable King dead. He was at large for a week but was finally tracked down in a barn at Tomachrochar, arrested, charged with culpable homicide and sentenced to 15 years, which he served at Peterhead Prison.

Constable King's grave can be seen in Abernethy Churchyard. He had previously been living in the Old Female School and after his death his widow and children continued to live there.

For many inhabitants, this must have been a golden era, a time when the Victorian spirit of entrepreneurism was able to thrive. One of these was my own great-grandfather, John Macaulay, (known locally as 'Old Macaula', the Gaelic pronunciation of his surname), whose name crops up in every aspect of village life. John was born at Dalvey Farm, Cromdale, in 1841. His father had come from Wester Ross to work as a farm labourer and had married Janet Smith from Abernethy. She was supposedly descended from William Smith of Rhinuie, the famous poacher and Gaelic poet – though the link may well be tenuous, as there seems to have been a tendency to embellish some of our family history! While John was still a child, the family moved to Old Bridge End and John started work in the forestry before going to Aberdeen to train as a master baker, walking over the hills there and back. On his return, he set up a bakery on the corner of Old Bridge End with Dell Road and later expanded the business into a butchery and general store. He married a local farmer's daughter, Grace Grant from Tombaie, and rented 30 acres of land on which he raised sheep and cattle for meat to sell in his shop. With the arrival of tourism, he started up a horse-and-carriage hiring business, which was particularly remunerative in transporting summer visitors to and from the station or taking them up into the hills on grand picnics. Music was another of his accomplishments. He held the post of 'leader of psalmody' in the parish church and taught the Sunday School children to sing Gaelic psalms for the 'kirk soiree' – or AGM. He was also a member of the early School Board. When land on Dell Road became available, he leased a large plot below the church on which he built the impressive villa of Badendossan for letting to rich families. Another plot further up the road was also acquired by the family and on it his brother Peter, a master mason also responsible for Tulloch School, built Hawthorn (now Morlich), with an impressive wall in front of it decorated by a stone ball and pyramid to show off his building skills.

    Not content with that, in 1898 John took over the lease of the farm of Lettoch, leaving his sons to run the family business. The Dowager Countess proposed to build a new, two-room dwelling house for the incoming tenant, but my great-grandfather made some kind of arrangement by which a large, four-bedroom house was built instead, again for letting to summer visitors.

He was also, as I discovered in my researches, involved in compiling the 1871 and 1881 censuses, entering with relish, in his neat copperplate handwriting, the details about himself, his family and his neighbours.

So for the village of Nethy Bridge, and the surrounding area of Abernethy, the Victorian years were a boom time, with the area benefitting enormously from the railway stations in its midst. Not until the 1960s did it experience such a dramatic expansion again.

Chapter 5

Nethy Bridge in Peace and at War – 1900-1945

In the years leading up to World War I, Nethy Bridge became a prosperous place. The visitors brought by the railway continued to arrive in droves. The local paper, *'The Strathspey Herald'*, carried lists of the visitors in residence, while local trades people did good business.

The 1901 census shows that the shop at Nethy Bridge House had become a post office as well as a grocer and draper. A postman, living in Cherry Cottage at the corner of Culvardie (now replaced by the house called Bowlins) was also employed to deliver mail to outlying areas. At the Causer, the blacksmith was now living in a house called Bynack View, probably the present-day Bynack, which may well may have existed without its name before that. Perhaps this was the house that started the fashion for calling houses after mountains – certainly, of all the Cairngorm range, Bynack has always also been considered as Nethy Bridge's special favourite. Looking at the house now, it is hard to understand how it justified its name, since the mountains are well obscured by surrounding trees and even without them the house hardly seems to be facing the right way! In the same census, Pine Cottage has appeared (called after a tree, as were so many of the earlier houses), still one of only a scattering of houses between Balnagowan and the Causer.

The Nethy Bridge Hotel, still being run by A.G. McKenzie with the assistance of his wife and daughter, was a grand affair, powered by 'the latest improved acetylene gas'. Visitors could be met on arrival at Broomhill Station by the hotel's own horse-drawn 'omnibus'. While there, they could take advantage of its 'wagonette' or could hire its 'New Argyle Motor car', complete with careful driver. Excursions to such places as Strathpeffer, the Falls of Foyers, Loch Laggan or Lochindorb would be charged at one shilling a mile. Or they could take any one of a number of walks around Craigmore, Carn na Loinne or Tulloch, with possible stops for tea at such houses as Lyngarrie and Backharn.

Visitors to the hotel could take a single room for four shillings and sixpence a night, a double room for seven shillings and a sitting-room for nine shillings a day, while their servants could board in the stewards' room for five shillings a day and have a bedroom for two shillings a night. For a fire or a bath, hot or cold, in the bathroom or bedroom, they paid extra and there were separate charges for breakfast, luncheon, tea (at 4p.m.) and dinner (at 7.30p.m.).

The hotel also had its own motor garage, 'specially designed for the purpose and equipped with inspection pit and washing stances'.

The village is recommended for its healthy climate, with 'eminent meteorologist' Dr Buchan quoted as saying: "The upper district of Strathspey represents the finest summer climate anywhere to be found in the British Isles"; while a certain Dr Martineau explains how a holiday on the West Coast of Scotland had brought on a fit of gout, while one in Strathspey had cured the condition. Another boast is of the great age of its inhabitants: "The natives generally live to a good old age. At the end of 1912 there were, living in a radius of a mile, twenty people between the ages of eighty and ninety-nine... some of the oldest of whom were able to go about their ordinary work." This latter comment may well have been inspired by a postcard of the time with a photo of 'Octogenarians at Nethy Bridge'. While it may well be true that some inhabitants were long-lived, there were many others who succumbed to the common diseases of the time, with TB being particularly rife. My own grandfather, who lived from 1875 to 1969, was one of eleven children of whom six died before reaching their thirties, not at all uncommon in the village at the time.

The spiritual needs of southern visitors were also looked after by Church of England services held in the Drill Hall during the summer season, in addition to the two Scottish churches – Free and Established.

A.G. McKenzie, who lived for a while in Birchfield, was also a pillar of the community, involved in other aspects of village life such as the Strathspey Farmers' Club and the School Board. The school itself continued to be under the charge of Andrew Steele until 1920, but in 1903 it acquired a pupil teacher who was to become familiar to generations of locals – Maggie Grant, Balnagowan. She left a few years later to go to training college, then taught at Auldearn before returning to teach at Abernethy as a 'certified teacher' in 1913. The vexed question of the water supply was once again tackled in 1909 when both school and school house were included in a new supply for the nearby manse (the House of Abernethy). Schoolmaster Andrew Steele decided that, since the supply was to be gravity fed, he might also install a hot water system in his home. There was further expansion of the school in 1910 with the building of a 'stone and lime house' for cooking and laundry work. At the same time a new stove was installed, for which Mr Steele had been agitating for some time, claiming in 1902 that it was 'impossible to heat the school with the present heating arrangements'. Cookery teaching was the province of Miss Taylor who, like Miss Grant, had begun as a pupil teacher but who was to remain at the school for many years. Classes in the apparently new subject of 'experimental science' were also introduced and there was talk of re-introducing the soup kitchen which had provided for the children in earlier years but which must at some point have been closed down. A suggestion of providing free school meals was however, not welcomed, in fact the School Board agreed unanimously to petition Parliament against the idea, presumably worried about the expense. They did though show concern about the children's health needs. Dr Barclay from Grantown regularly visited the school and it was arranged that those requiring 'stopping teeth and extractions' would be seen by a visiting dentist from Elgin. In 1912 there was talk that the Nursing Association wanted to take over the Old Female School for a residential nurse and this did finally come about in 1918. The education authorities retained ownership of the house for many more years, with the school janitor Jim Fraser living there in the 1960s.

An interesting request was made by the Abernethy School Board in 1902 to the Parish Council of Glasgow, requesting funds because; 'the Board were under necessity of providing more accommodation, desks and apparatus for the addition of children from Glasgow to the Glenbrown district' It was claimed that of 24 children in the school there at the time, 17 were from Glasgow. A few years later, it was also estimated that a quarter of all the pupils in Abernethy Public School were 'paupers from Glasgow'. This is an acknowledgement of the large number of 'Glasgow orphans' or 'boarded out boys' who arrived in the area throughout the 19th and early 20th centuries as part of a Government policy to remove impoverished children from the city slums and bring them up in the healthier atmosphere of the Highlands. These children were boarded out, most often on farms, and were expected to work for their keep. Many were treated harshly, seen more as a resource than as a charitable cause. Some returned to the cities or took part in emigration schemes to Canada or Australia, but many remained in and around Nethy Bridge and became valuable members of the community, with several of them still resident here today, having married and raised families in the area.

The Highland Games continued to thrive on its site at Coulnakyle, handily between the GNSR (Great North of Scotland Railway) station of Broomhill and the HR (Highland Railway) station of Nethy Bridge, with special trains being laid on to transport visitors from Speyside and Aberdeen. A poster from 1910 advertises entry prices of 2/6 (12½) for 'motors and carriages (occupants excluded)', which suggests that the motor car was gradually making its presence felt among the horse-drawn carriages – and for those with neither of these means of transport, there was also a 'bicycle store on the ground'. Apart from the parking charge, visitors could pay 2/6 for the Grand Stand, 2/- for a reserved seat or 1/- for other parts, while children paid just 3d. There were also 'temperance refreshments and luncheon to be had on the ground'.

More houses were being built, including Lily Bank in 1904, opposite the football field, constructed by and for a local builder. This was later to be renamed Granlea, then Garlogie (by the Christie family who had owned a farm at Garlogie in Aberdeen-shire) and finally Tigh na Fraoch. The Police Station beside it (now Aspen Lodge) also seems to have been built at around the same time. For the next 70 years, it was to be home to a series of local 'bobbies' and their families, all very much part of the community. It also housed a cell where prisoners might be kept overnight. If their crimes warranted it, they might then be moved on to Inverness, but there is no record of serious crime in Nethy Bridge since the murder of Thomas King in 1898.

A new departure were the grander, more individually-designed houses being built by rich industrialists from the cities, for use as summer residences. Families and servants arrived, generally by train, at the start of the summer while the businessman owner, unable to take such a long break, would come to and fro at weekends.

Lewis Grant, who is described as an engineer from Kirkcaldy, the linoleum town, took out a feu on an irregular strip of land across the road, and further along from, Balnagowan. The Dowager Countess was prepared to allow him to build a house there, but with strict instructions that it must be built of stone and lime with a roof of slate or tiles. There could be a fence in front of it, or a dyke of stone and lime but this must not be more than four and a half feet high. There was to be no steam engine there, or any other industry likely to cause a nuisance, and on no account was it to be used for the sale of 'spirituous liquors'. The result, in 1911, was the magnificent, Tudoresque mansion called Ardavon, overlooking the River Nethy from the top of a steep bank. Early pictures show that it commanded a clear view of the Cairngorms, unobstructed by the many trees which later grew up in gardens on either side of the Nethy, while on the other side it looked straight across open farmland. It is interesting to note that Lewis Grant's address in Kirkcaldy is 'Lettoch' suggesting, perhaps, an earlier connection with the village.

Along the road between Nethy Bridge and the Golf Course, the Dunan (now the Mount View Hotel) was built by a Mr Fraser for his new bride. Allegedly when she saw it, she complained that it was too big so he was forced to move her to another, smaller house at the family home of Mondhuie. The Frasers were the parents of Margaret and Jessie Fraser who were to be well known, years later, as teachers in Nethy and Grantown schools and their brother Harry, who tragically died in World War II. On Margaret's death in the 1990s, she left a legacy to the Community Centre which allowed for improvements to the hall and tennis courts. Meanwhile the Dunan was acquired by Dr P. Watkin Brown. The Grey House was built for Mr Cromelyn Brown and may have been designed by Edinburgh architect Robert Lorimer. Later it was to become a temperance hotel, owned by a Grant family.

Tigh na Torr (House on the Hillock) was built, fittingly, at the top of the Church Brae, across the road from the Free Church. Forest House, a magnificent, balconied, wooden building originally known as Forest Home, appeared in the forest close to the nursery and round the back of

Heatherbrae. It was to be used throughout the 1950s and 1960s as the summer home of Neville Davidson, minister of Glasgow Cathedral.

Aultmore House, on the side of Craigmore and beside the burn of the same name, was built for Archibald Merrielees whose family had made their fortune in Russia. His father and partner (a Mr Muir) had founded the M and M department store in Moscow. It was designed by English architect Quenelle. The house was sold in 1922 to the Nivisson family (including Lord Glendyne), who extended it and retained it until the early 1970s.

In 1905, Balnagowan sawmill, previously part of Balnagowan farm, was taken over by a new tenant, Alexander McPherson who was a carpenter as well as a sawmiller. He also became undertaker, making some of the coffins himself and having others delivered by railway from Dundee. The McPherson family continued to run the mill until it closed in the 1960s.

In 1910, Forest Lodge was taken over by shooting tenant Richard Holt, whose father had been shooting in the Abernethy Forest, staying at Dell Lodge, as far back as 1868. The Holt family were wealthy cotton brokers from Liverpool and owned the Blue Funnel shipping line. One of the Holt daughters married into the Naylor family who continued to rent the lodge, remaining as shooting tenants and later owners, right up to 1988 when it was bought over by the RSPB. The family still maintain a presence in the area, with one son, Murray, retaining the cottage at Lyngarrie and another, Christopher, owning Rynettin.

Fasga na Coille was built in the woods behind Balnagowan for Miss Annie Bannatyne, later to be taken over by Miss Annie Holt, a daughter of the Forest Lodge family. Miss Bannatyne, along with a Miss Hall were responsible for funding the building of the Village Institute, nowadays called the Community Centre, near the foot of Dell Road. The building appears to have been erected initially in 1905, but in 1911 it was handed over to the community to be the responsibility of a group of trustees. These comprised the village schoolmaster, the ministers of both Church of Scotland and Free Church of Scotland, the chairman of the parish council and the medical officer of health of the parish – an arrangement which was to continue for the next 100 years, being the responsibility of a long procession of people with these or similar titles.

Between that building and the main road through the village, John Taylor built his general store which was to develop into the shop and Post Office of today. The centre of the village had finally taken shape. John had two daughters, Rose and Ella, so when he built himself a house beside the shop he called it Rosella – a name which has aroused much curiosity over the years.

The Dowager Countess of Seafield died in 1911 and, since she had no direct heir, the estate passed to her great-nephew Captain James Ogilvie-Grant and, after his death in 1915 (killed by a sniper during World War I), to his only child, Nina who became the Countess of Seafield. The chiefship of Clan Grant, however, could only be passed down a male line, so his brother Sir Trevor Ogilvie-Grant became Lord Seafield along with the title of Lord Strathspey.

Community life flourished in these pre-war years. An amateur dramatic society was well supported, putting on plays and musicals. A 1914 photograph of the Nethy Bridge Dramatic Company by Grantown photographer A. Ledingham shows an impressively large cast of men, women and children, who had performed the musical drama, 'Prince Charlie', by Aberdeenshire writer Gavin Greig. The cast included familiar local names such as Kennedy and Macaulay. According to the caption, "This was regarded on all hands as a very successful performance."

There was a significant break from the past in 1912, when church minister Duncan Robertson retired, as he was the last to preach in Gaelic. Although people were still speaking the language among themselves, particularly in the more rural areas, all the children were being taught English at school and this was apparently seen as the language of the future, necessary for communicating with all the newcomers and holiday-makers in the village. When the post of a new minster was advertised, it was stated that Gaelic was 'desirable but not absolutely necessary'.

The outbreak of World War I in August 1914 brought about the end to much of the entertainment, signified by the immediate cancellation of the Grantown Show and the Nethy Games. Although the Show was re-introduced between the wars, the Games were not to resurface until 1946, in a very different world. As with everywhere else in the country, Nethy Bridge lost many of its young men who signed up at the Drill Hall to join the famous Scottish regiments and marched proudly away, some of them never to return.

However, Nethy Bridge prospered during World War I through its forestry which was still a thriving industry, managed up to 1912 by John Stephen and thereafter by his son-in-law William Marshall. He had moved here from the Novar Estate in Ross-shire in 1912, taking over Dell Cottage and the forester's croft in Dell Road where he kept some stock and some bees, as well as looking after the Nursery. Mr Marshall was a well-known figure in the area as he was an expert in all aspects of wildlife and it was to him that people came when they had questions about flora and fauna. Later, he was to write a regular column for the *Northern Scot* newspaper, 'From a Glen Window', under the pen-name of his favourite mountain, Mam Suim.

The war meant that Britain could no longer import timber from abroad and, since so much planting had been going on in Abernethy throughout the 1800s, the area was in a good position to supply the wood so desperately needed for both military and industrial use. Timber could now be transported by rail, but getting it from the forests to the stations presented a new challenge, since floating down the burns had been stopped, partly because of protests by angling interests. The solution was to build tram lines throughout the forests and two new railway sidings where the timber could be loaded on to the mainline railways. One of these sidings, a few hundred yards to the north of the station, was known as the 'German siding', because the track leading to it was built by German prisoners-of-war, who also carried out the work of felling the trees in the forest known as the 'Lettoch plantation' and transporting the timber on wagons. The track ran from the station across a field where Broomhill Court now stands, then to the Causer where it turned up by Badanfhuarain and across the moor to the edge of the Lettoch fields, known as the Drums. This was in the middle of the 'Lettoch plantation' and it was from here that the trees were taken – mostly for the making of pit props. The track was made of wooden timbers, about 15cm in diameter, laid on round logs and secured with large iron nails. The trucks were also made of wood with iron axles bolted on and wheels attached. When full of logs, these were pushed by the Germans towards the station, helped by gravity since it was mainly downhill, but more effort was required to push them back uphill when empty. Marks of the railway can still be seen in places – for example, where it was built up to cross a boggy area at the end of the Lettoch fields. The wooden rails were taken up after 1918 to be used for other building projects or firewood but the huge iron nails could still be found occasionally in the 1960s.

The German prisoner-of-war camp was at Lynstock, where Lynstock Park now stands, and residents have found stones used in its construction. There does not appear to have been too much anti-German feeling in the village at the time, in fact many of the men made wooden toys and presented them to local children. Their food supplies were augmented by loads of horseflesh, delivered regularly at the station. Their presence was also welcomed at the end of the war when they helped to put out a major forest fire which destroyed a vast area of the Abernethy Forest between Dell Farm and Lynamer in Tulloch. The houses in Dell Road (then known as Seafield Place) were evacuated as it was feared the fire might spread to the village. The area was reforested in 1926.

Another railway siding, about half a mile south of the station near Tomachrochar, was known as the 'Canadian siding,' as this was used by Canadian foresters who had been brought into the area to help replace local men who were fighting abroad. They had a camp at Raeduack, in the forest near Tulloch. Their forestry operations were a much more sophisticated affair centred on a large, well-organised sawmill, driven by a steam engine.

A narrow-gauge railway was built to transport the timber to the siding, with the carriages pulled at first by horses, later by flat-faced 'puggy' engines, leading to them being called 'puggy' lines. The operation continued for some time after the war, run by the Board of Trade. There was also supposed to have been a camp of Finnish forestry workers, close to the Canadian camp.

In this way large areas of trees were cleared, on the side of Craigmore hill, on the moor above Lettoch and in the Thomson's Brae area between Dell and Forest Lodge. They were not reforested until the great planting schemes of the late 1960s and, in the meantime, there flourished great crops of cranberries eagerly picked by locals to make jam. Local people would also take their wheelbarrows into the areas to collect 'crackers' – the dead branches left on the trees after felling – for firewood, while wood from the tram lines no longer in use was taken to build such things as sheep pens. One tree which escaped the mass felling – and others before it – was the giant of the forest known as Peter Porter's tree, on the side of Craigmore, said to be more than 250 years old when it finally rotted away within the last 20 years. This magnificent Scots pine was supposed to have been named after one of the porters who ferried people across the Spey at Balliefurth and local legend had it that, when the woodsmen approached to chop it down, a voice came out of the tree warning them to leave. With the trees felled all around it, its outline could be clearly seen from as far away as the Lettoch Road and it was a popular destination for Sunday-afternoon walks from the village.

Children were given dispensation from school in September to help with the wartime harvests, while many of the women played their part by collecting the sphagnum moss that grew in damp places around the forest and sending it off to be used as dressings for wounded soldiers. Even Nethy Bridge horses had to do their bit for the war effort. There is a story that William Macaulay, who was still involved with the family carriage-hiring business at Culvardie, heard that men had arrived on the train to requisition horses. He rushed to the stables, where they had one remarkably intelligent horse called Polly. Since the family also tenanted the farm at Lettoch, he

Abernethy Church, also known as the East Church, pictured in the 1930s

World War II Canadian Camp on the Garlyne Road

World War I Canadian Timber Camp at Raedvack

Donnie MacKenzie

Gathering Spagnum Moss during World War I

Katie Grant's cottage at the top of Clachaig Brae, in the 1920s

MDC MacKenzie's shop in the 1960s with staff

Nethy Bridge Church on Dell Road (previously the Free Church)

Pre World War II view of Nethy House, Nethy Bridge Hotel and Tigh na Drochaid

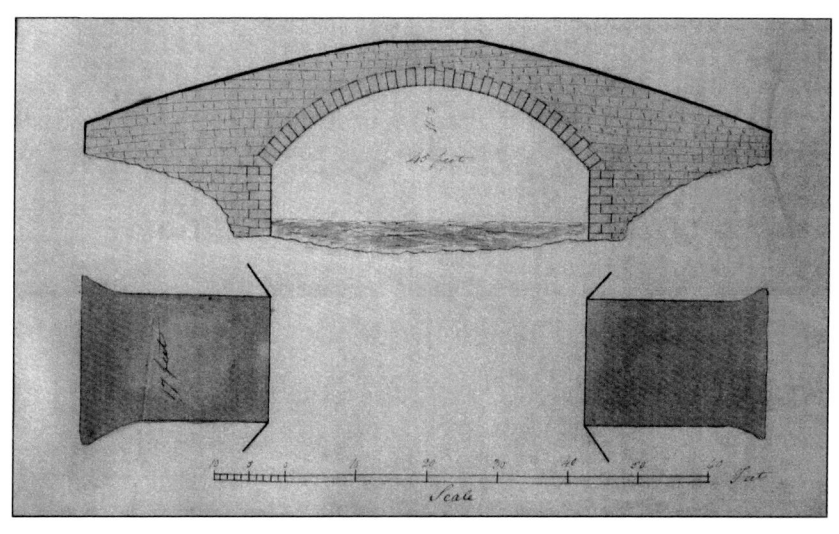

Sketch for the 1771 bridge over the Nethy, drawn up at Castle Grant

Station Road in the late 1940s, showing the fish shop, Rose Cottage, Walter Grant's shop and the end of Nethy House

The Drill Hall, 1940s

The Hangman's Tree at Lynstock, being felled in the 1970s (A McCook)

The Nethy Bridge Hotel, before the 1930s

The original Abernethy Manse - now home to the Abernethy Trust

The Thieves' Pass

W. Grant's shoemaker's, Station Road

Walter Grant's grocery shop

William MacDonald, wood merchant - he built Heatherbrae

World War I timber railway in the Lettoch Plantation

World War I German POW forestry workers at Nethy Bridge

Driving north: The A9 main road over Drumochter Pass in the early 20th century

Forest Lodge c1900

Ardavon (A. McCook)

Badendossan (A. McCook)

Balnagowan Mill in the 1960s (A. McCook)

Castle Roy, one of the oldest Castles in Scotland (S McCook)

Coulnakyle (A. McCook)

Heatherbrae (A. McCook)

Nethy Bridge in winter (S McCook)

Nethy Bridge village (S McCook)

Abernethy Church from Castle Moy (S McCook)

released Polly, took her out on to Dell Road and shouted the name of the farm. Polly set off at a gallop and was thus saved the fate of the war horses. Unfortunately Polly's companion Dolly was not so lucky and was taken away on the train.

The village did recover somewhat between the wars. More houses were built, particularly in the area between Balnagowan and the Causer. Clachbheo was built by 1920 and occupied by a family called Livingstone, supposedly related to Dr Livingstone the missionary and explorer. The house name literally means 'living stone'. Grianach was built in 1936 and bought by Miss Gladys Younger, of the Younger brewery family, an indomitable lady who lived there until the 1980s, having been president of the village WRI for much of that time. The Neuk was built at the crossroads for James McPherson, brother of Jock, who had taken over Balnagowan sawmill from his father Alexander – the name, meaning corner, being used by locals to identify the area until a subsequent owner changed it to Meall a Bhuachaille.

Money was raised from local people and summer visitors to employ a district nurse and a cottage was built for her half way up the Church brae. This continued to be occupied by nurses until the NHS sold it off in the early 1980s and its name was subsequently changed to Dornie.

Meanwhile up at the Causer, the first of the council houses (referred to at the time as 'the new houses') were built in 1934 – the row of semi-detached bungalows– numbers 1 to 16 Lynstock Crescent. 'Lynstock' means 'Meadow of the Tree Stumps', suggesting that the forest had been cleared here at a much earlier date to provide a field for the farm of Lynstock. At around the same time, a new blacksmith took over at the smiddy – Jim MacDonald who hailed from Kiltarlity where he had learned his trade from his father, before becoming a motor mechanic during World War I. He was kept busy, as there were still plenty of working horses to be shod.

It is an interesting point that, although impressive stone-and-slate buildings had been a feature of Nethy Bridge for decades, many residents were still living in much more basic homes, such as the croft house of Katy Grant, at the top of the Clachaig brae, where Tigh Sithe now stands. Her turf-walled, heather-thatched house had a cow-shed attached to the side, with a door from one to the other meaning that she did not have to go outside to milk the cow. My uncle remembers visiting her in the 1920s and being impressed by how clean and neat her cottage was, in fact she had at one time won a Strathspey Farmers' Club award for the best-kept cottage in the area. Katy Grant also did the laundry for the people at Forest Lodge, across the Nethy, which may be the reason the bridge behind the lodge was always known as the Laundry Bridge – though it is more likely that it acquired its name because the laundry was carried out there, in the Nethy beside the bridge.

Children still attended Abernethy Public School up to the leaving age of 14, with the schoolmasters at the time being John Scott who had taken over from Andrew Steele in 1920, and later, Kenneth Fraser. Those who passed the 'qualifying' exam, could study such subjects as French and Latin, but if they wished to advance to the Higher Leaving Certificate they had to transfer, at the age of 14, to Grantown Grammar School, travelling there by bike or train. Grace Smith remembers how in the late 1930s she and her friends would assemble at the Causer in the morning, ready for the 45-minute cycle trip to Grantown. Only in winter, if the weather was particularly bad, would they take the train, which still involved a lengthy walk at the other end, from Grantown's East Station across the Spey Bridge and into the town. Ten years later, Rita Templeton remembers travelling there by a newly introduced service bus but having to take the train home, leaving school before the last period and hurrying to catch it because if the train was missed, it meant a long walk home.

Transport moved at a very different pace from that of today. Although the train could bring travellers into the area at a reasonable speed, travel by road was a different story. Even the A9 was mostly untarred and Jean Munro, whose family drove north from Edinburgh each summer, to take a house for the season in the 1920s and 1930s, describes them usually breaking the journey with an overnight stop.

The Nethy Bridge Hotel was taken over by Mrs Fotheringham, a formidable lady whose business empire had begun with a railway station book stall at Aviemore. She went on to run hotels in Inverness and Lairg, and rented the farm of Coulnakyle, which was used to grow vegetables to supplement the hotel meals. Although her reputation among the staff was as a strict disciplinarian, those who encountered her as friends and neighbours found her to be nothing but kind. The hotel was expanded with the creation of a large new wing and a lift installed which is still in use today – reputedly still satisfying building regulations in 2012. Throughout World War II, when there cannot have been many people taking holidays, it continued to advertise itself as, 'Situated at the foot of the Cairngorms – Ideal Hotel for Mountaineers – facilities for River and Loch Fishing, Golf, Tennis. Excellent Centre for Motoring.'

The hotel was not the only place taking advantage of the advent of the motor car. At Culvardie, the Macaulays' horse-hiring business and stables were converted to a taxi service and garages, run by son James, who conveyed passengers to and from Nethy Bridge or Broomhill Stations by car. The wooden garages can still be seen, on the right as you walk up the Culvardie road, just behind the Old Bakery.

Community life was going strong and the large hall which is now the main part of the Community Centre was built in the 1930s, with help from the Carnegie Trust. One of the organisations to make good use of it was the Abernethy branch of the Scottish Women's Rural Institute (SWRI), which was formed in 1936. The original Women's Institute had been founded in Canada in 1897 and the Scottish version in 1917. Both very firmly rooted in agriculture, it provided a chance for farmers' wives and daughters to socialise with others and perfect the crafts of sewing and baking so central to their existence. In Nethy Bridge the organisation was seen by some as rather frivolous in comparison to the Church Women's Guild. It was to become a very big part of village life, however, being instrumental in organising Halloween and Christmas parties for the village children, as well as events for its senior citizens.

For the young people, in their teens or twenties, hill-walking seems to have been a very popular pastime. Lacking motor transport, they used bikes to travel as far into the hills as possible, often to Pitfianich Bothy far up Nethy side, then perhaps camping there as they made expeditions up Bynack, Cairngorm, Ben Macdhuie or further Munros.

Of course the years of peace were to be interrupted once more in 1939 with the outbreak of World War II, the first manifestation of which in Nethy Bridge was a flood of evacuees. Many of them disappeared within a month or two, returning to the cities as the expected bombing did not start immediately. Other evacuees, especially those who came with their families, were to remain in the area throughout the war and sometimes even beyond, becoming a part of the community.

Nethy Bridge became a centre for various camps, both for forestry work and army training. The Canadian Forestry Corps had their huts and sawmill in the School Wood, beside the Garlyne Road and behind present-day Dirdhu Court. Until the late 1960s, when the area was replanted with trees, it was a large, bare space where youngsters used to play and even today an investigation can discover piles of sawdust left over from the wartime forestry operations. As D-Day approached the fitter among these Canadians, who were part of the Canadian Army, left Scotland to fight on the Continent. Another camp, on the left side of Dell Road, just after Dell Farm, was occupied by the Newfoundland Forestry Corps, known fondly as 'The Newfies'. They saw themselves as rivals of the other Canadian foresters – resulting in regular fights between the two sets of men. Later, the same area served as a camp for German prisoners-of-war, many of whom went out to help on farms in the area. Some remained after the end of the war and there was one case where a local man, returning from years of incarceration in a German prisoner-of-war camp, was horrified to find one of the enemy working on his home farm. On the other hand, another returning local befriended the two Germans who were working at his home and remained in correspondence with them for the rest of his life.

From 1940, Forest Lodge was a base for the Norwegian Special Operations Executive, a company of Norwegians who had managed to escape from their country after it was invaded by the Nazis. Trained by Captain Martin Linge, who died early in the war, they were also known as Kompani Linge, and their other bases included Glenmore Lodge and Drumintoul, Coylumbridge. They were being trained as Commandos and saboteurs who were then sent back to Norway on special missions either by boat or parachuted in from planes. One of the best known and most successful operations was to blow up the heavy water plant at Telemark, thus preventing Germany from developing nuclear bombs. The famous film of the raid, I am told, bears little resemblance to the reality! Alistair McCook, who was a boy in Nethy Bridge at the time, recalls that the Norwegians used to appear at village dances or at the films which were provided by a mobile unit at the community centre. Then they would disappear for around six months at a time. They have also left their mark in the building housing the dog kennels at Forest Lodge, which was used as cells for misdemeanours, in the form of Norwegian graffiti and some really clever sketches on the walls. There is even a sketch of Norwegian King Haakon, who visited them there at the time.

The Abernethy Forest and the Cairngorms were a training ground not only for the Norwegians but also for the British RASC regiment, as well as a regiment of turban-wearing Indian soldiers, who provided an exotic sight for locals as they moved, along with hundreds of mules, around Tulloch and Kincardine Moor. At one point US soldiers were also billeted at Forest Lodge.

While most of the regular soldiers lived in camps, others, including the officers, were billeted in houses all over the village. Any house which happened to be empty – holiday homes or those whose owners were away doing war work - was used for this purpose. Mrs Edie Robertson remembers that while her family lived at Seafield Place, there were young soldiers billeted next door at Fir Knowe (now Talisker). She remembers her mother taking pity on them, young lads away from home for the first time, and used to bring them boiling water to shave in every morning. Aultmore House was used as a nursing home for wounded soldiers.

There was also a massive ammunition dump at Loch Garten, guarded by the soldiers. For the youngsters, these were exciting times. Mona Cameron recalls encountering soldiers involved in exercises around her childhood summer home at Tulloch and joining in with them as a game, telling one group of soldiers where their colleagues were hiding. The dump was to spark yet another major forest fire, destroying trees from Loch Garten to Nethy Bridge before being put out by a gang of local volunteers.

The village also had its Home Guard unit made up, as in the popular TV series 'Dad's Army', of men too old or too young to fight in the war, as well as those in reserved occupations such as farming. The stories they told, of creating extra holes in Nethy Golf Course during hand grenade practice, and of rounding up the men for a night-time exercise but telling one to stay and put on the kettle, so they could all have 'a nice cup of tea' before they set out, shows that the popular TV series was not far from the mark. They also had their own 'Corporal Jones' character, in Lewie Grant, who had been in the previous war and knew how things should be done, and perhaps their 'Sergeant Pike' in a very young Alistair McCook.

With all the strangers in the village and so many men away to the war, it is not surprising that there were quite a few romances, some of which outlasted the years of the war. Dances were held in the village hall, as well as cinema shows which were operated from a mobile unit outside. Some local girls married Canadians, with some emigrating with them after the war.

The war brought some lasting changes to the village. Perhaps it was the shortage of labour on the farms that forced them to become more mechanized but by the end of the war, tractors had gradually taken over from horses. The water-powered meal mill on the Aultmore at the Garlyne, to which the farmers had all transported their oats to be ground into oatmeal, closed down, although it remained in the ownership of the Gordon family, who had been millers there for two previous generations. The mill continued to be used as a farm outbuilding until recently, when it was converted into a house.

A host of new shops had sprung up, while some of the older ones had closed. The bakery at Culvardie had continued to be run by a series of shopkeepers including Mr Hume and Geordie West, finally closing down soon after the end of the war. Fresh milk was supplied from Nethy Bridge's own dairy farm in the fields beyond Culvardie, run by Richard and his son Jimmy George from their house, Fairview. They used several fields throughout the village as grazing, including the Church glebe and Balnagowan, and their herd of around 14 Ayrshire cows were a regular sight being driven through the village every day at milking time. Also in Culvardie was Mr Stubbert's shoemaker's shop, though he later moved to the village. He is said to have been the first person to install electricity into his home but this came to an end when, during a thunder storm, a fire broke out in the kitchen doing a fair amount of damage.

Granite Cottage, behind the Village Institute, became a grocer's shop run by Fergus Robertson It was later taken over by the Co-op, under which it existed as three separate departments: grocer, butcher and draper, until the 1960s. Along at Duack Bridge, Miss Methven (daughter of the original occupant) still ran a bakery with Francis Doull, a brother-in-law, baking the bread from a shed at the back. Miss Methven is remembered as an elegant elderly lady with silver hair and a black velvet choker around her neck. Not forgetting her family's religious roots, she often handed out religious pamphlets with the bread.

Before World War II, the Post Office was in the present-day Nethy House, then a shop owned by Wilson and Parr. Across the bridge John Taylor had his general store while his daughter also ran a tearoom in the summer. All this changed, with the arrival of MDC MacKenzie, more familiarly known as 'Donnie', who was to become a local legend. Donnie, whose family came from Ross-shire, took over Mr Taylor's shop and incorporated the Post

Office within it and this soon became the hub of the village – the place to which everyone came if they wanted information or advice. Donnie, a rather sophisticated gentleman, was also to become county councillor. Donnie's rather less sophisticated brother, 'Willie Butcher', opened a butcher's shop across the road at Caberfeidh, while their sister Mamie was for many years the village nurse.

Across the bridge, on the road leading down to the station, were several more shops. Mr McAndrew was a tailor. He was very crippled and used a tricycle to get about, but he was able to sit cross-legged on his bench to sew his clothes. Next to that was Curry's the Chemist, an offshoot of a Grantown shop – it did not have its own pharmacist, but people could collect their prescriptions there or buy over-the-counter medicines. Then there was Gregor Grant (known as 'Boss'), the shoemaker, who later moved to Juniper Cottage at Duack Bridge where he had a prominent sign: 'Boots Repaired Here Free of Charge Tomorrow'. These shops also served a social function with men dropping in for a gossip, a discussion or a 'news', sometimes even a game of draughts, and they often stayed open in the evening for this purpose. Further down the road was a surgery, used by Grantown-based Dr Barclay, and still further down, beyond Rose Cottage (occupied by the George family) and just before the station, was a fish shop run by Mrs 'Fish' Murray. She is remembered as a big, powerful, Gaelic-speaking woman who would brook no nonsense but had, nevertheless, a good sense of humour. Fresh fish was delivered every day on the train from Aberdeen and this shop also sold sweeties and had a tearoom, used mainly by forestry workers. Across Station Road, on the site of the present-day butcher, was a grocery owned by Walter Grant, then William Gall, later taken over by Coopers.

There was also a shop at the Causer, run by Mrs McAndrew, wife of the tailor. Among the usual groceries she sold sweets and broken biscuits, much appreciated by children on their way to school. The McAndrew family owned a croft at the Causer on the other side of the road from Causer Cottages, now occupied by various houses and housing estates.

It may seem strange now that so many shops could have existed in so small a community, but this was a different era, before the age of the city superstores. Very few people had a car and no one owned a freezer so they bought fresh food every day, taking their time to chat as they shopped – a different, less hectic way of life. And for those in outlying parts for whom even a trip to the shops in Nethy Bridge was a luxury, there were the vans which delivered news along with the groceries. Vans came from Grantown and Boat of Garten as well as Nethy Bridge shops such as the Co-op and Cooper's, the latter driven by popular Nethy Bridge resident Tommy MacPherson. Mona Cameron remembers that in Tulloch at this time they were visited by a van every day – and sometimes two in one day.

The Abernethy Parish Council – forerunner of today's Community Council – was formed in 1943, replacing a previous Amenities Committee and aimed to deal with all matters of importance throughout the parish. At the original meeting was the minister, Ian McAllister, schoolmaster Kenneth Fraser, George MacKenzie, Tigh na Drochaid (garage owner and son of the previous hotel proprietor) and Mrs Margaret Grant, Dalbuiack.

Of all the periods of Nethy Bridge's history, it is easiest to become misty-eyed and nostalgic about the years immediately after the war, with a strong sense of community and so many facilities at hand. Nothing remains the same however, in Nethy Bridge as in the rest of the world. The 1960s were on the horizon, about to bring another period of boom and transformation.

Chapter 6

1945-1970 – Post-War, the Rise of Aviemore and Winter Sports

The post-war years may have been a period of austerity throughout Britain, but in Nethy Bridge it also seems to have been a time of great energy and enthusiasm. People who were around then talk of these as golden years, when everyone knew everyone else, children played together in 'Meggie Murray's Park' (the area between Dell Road and Forest House, where houses were built from the late 1960s onwards). Grown-ups got together at the weekly dances in the Community Centre or just at each others' homes where impromptu 'ceilidhs' would start up, with tea or whisky, a bite to eat, plenty of conversation and more often than not some music and singing.

For young people, the focal point of the village was the bridge where they would gather on summer evenings, sitting on the parapet or standing in the middle of the road to exchange gossip. Motor traffic was few and far between and travelled considerably more slowly than today. Or they would meet on the football pitch behind the village hall, to cheer on their local team which competed in the Strathspey league. It was said that a particular group of the footballers' wives and girlfriends were so vociferous that they struck terror into the heart of visiting referees.

The end of the war brought a great burst of community spirit. The village hall or institute was renamed the Community Centre and a Community Centre committee was formed with a representative from each organization in the village. Under its auspices, the Abernethy Highland Games was revived having been in abeyance since the start of World War I. This was a real community undertaking, for and by the village. The field at Coulnakyle being no longer available, they decided to hold the new Games in the heart of the village, on the football pitch. This, however was in poor condition so the locals, under the control of Golf Course groundsman A.S. Grant, set about stripping the turf, levelling and draining the field and re-laying the turf, using only the fairly basic machinery at hand. The result was an instant success. Competitors and spectators travelled from miles around to attend the first revived Nethy Games and it has retained its popularity ever since.

Another crowd puller was the Sheepdog Trials started by a group of local farmers, shepherds and other enthusiasts. It was held in a field at Tomdhu, and became part of the circuit which brought sheepdog-handlers from all over Scotland. There was a particular rush to have this event up and running by 1946, as word had reached the organisers that the Strathspey Farmers' Club had a plan to hold a sheepdog trials at Grantown. This organisation had managed to ride out both the wars, although no cattle shows had been held during the actual war years. With the declaration of peace, they were anxious to get going once more, but had decided it would not be feasible to organise a full show within a year, so a sheepdog trials might be a reasonable compromise. They were pipped at the post however by their rivals and the Nethy Bridge Sheepdog trials became a popular event in the summer diary.

The Games committee also organised an annual Burns night at which small plays were performed, with Nethy people dressing up as characters from the bard's life. The village coalman, Gordon Mackintosh, made an excellent Robert Burns, apparently, owing to physical similarities.

Highland dancing lessons were given by Elsie Ross in the little two-roomed house on Dell Road which she shared with her elderly mother. The house was later replaced by a much larger one, called Rowcliffe and then Craineag. It is interesting to note that its garage occupies the site – and is probably not much smaller than – the house where a generation of Nethy children learned to dance. The tradition of teaching Highland dancing was later to be carried on by one of Elsie Ross's pupils, Hilda Thomson (daughter of railway surfaceman Mr Watt).

At the same time, the face of the village was changed by the building of the majority of the council houses at Lynstock and MacKenzie Crescent. Numbers 1 to 16 Lynstock Crescent, the bungalows at the Causer end, had already been built in 1934, but the main batch was constructed in 1947 – large, solid, two-storey family homes, built in a crescent shape with a grassy communal area in front. This was one large-scale housing scheme about which there was no objection, as it was recognised that there was a real need for decent houses, weatherproof and supplied with running water, and all were occupied by local families. MacKenzie Crescent, named after the local shopkeeper, postmaster and councillor MDC MacKenzie, was added in the 1950s and electricity was a very early addition. It took longer though for power to reach the more outlying farms. Most of these were connected in the early 1960s but some very isolated places took longer to install even running water.

The raising of the school leaving age to 15 heralded a change in the make-up of Abernethy School. Whereas it had previously provided an academic secondary education including French, Latin and science to those who passed the 'qualifying' exam, it was now changed to a more vocational syllabus with technical subjects for the boys and domestic science for the girls. Those who passed the 'qualifying' at the age of 12 could move on to Grantown Grammar at that stage. A school bus was provided which brought secondary pupils from Carrbridge and Boat of Garten to Abernethy Junior Secondary, then picking up Nethy pupils and taking them on (along with some of the Boat of Garten scholars) to Grantown. Carrbridge pupils attending Grantown School had a more direct bus route. Since the road between the village and the Causer was too narrow for buses, Nethy pupils congregated at the bus shelter in the village. In reality, many pupils who had passed the exam opted to stay on at Nethy since they saw no use for higher education, knowing there were still jobs available, particularly in farming, forestry or the building industry.

Agriculture was still the chief employer in the area. When I attended the primary section of Abernethy School, from 1958 to 1965, five out of the nine pupils in my class were from farms - two of us the children of tenant farmers, three the children of farm workers. Most farmers were able to employ at least one worker while the big farms beside the Spey provided cottages for several families, often with a number of children. Tomdhu and Auchernack (on the Grantown road but still within Abernethy parish) had become dairy farms with the large, black-and-white Friesian cattle supplying milk for the village and beyond. Others, such as Rothiemoon and Coulnakyle, were still producing beef cattle, a mix of Aberdeen-Angus and Shorthorn, while higher up in Dorback and Tulloch were black-faced sheep which flourished on rough hill grazing. In between were the mixed farms with both cattle and sheep.

The farmers still grew oats but no longer for their own consumption. After threshing, the grain was fed to poultry and sometimes to calves; the chaff was used to line the hen houses and the straw as winter bedding for the cattle. Barley was also grown on some farms, the grain sold to the distilleries on Speyside, from which the farmers bought back 'draff' for cattle feed, the grains which had been used for whisky and which gave off a rich, malty smell.

Farming was still a sociable activity, with neighbours coming together for sheep gatherings and clippings, 'leading' (taking in the grain harvest) and threshing mills. Things were very slowly becoming mechanised as tractors replaced horses and a host of new implements took to the fields with names such as acrobats, wufflers, tedders, balers and finally, combine harvesters.

In later years with the new fashion for 'conservation', farmers were to be demonised as people who destroyed wildlife. Traditional farming methods were very much in tune with nature, encouraging a rich diversity of flora and fauna in the harvest fields, the pasture land, the moors and hills. Most farmers had a good appreciation and knowledge of the flowers and birds on their land and it was to them that early botanists and ornithologists who visited the area would look for information.

Ornithology took on a whole new dimension in 1954 with the return of the osprey to Speyside. This impressive fish-eating bird of prey had once been common throughout the British Isles but was believed to have become extinct by 1916. A breeding pair from Scandinavia found their way to the forest on the Abernethy side of Loch Garten and the RSPB moved in, constructing a viewing hide with binoculars where the public could come and watch the birds on their nest. This proved a popular draw for visitors to the area and has continued to be so as ospreys have continued to use the same nest up to the present day.

Forestry was also going strong with a great demand for timber after the depredations of two wars. Much work went on under the able leadership of head foresters William Marshall, Johnnie MacDonald, Donald Carr and, finally, Jimmy MacLeod. It was a healthy, outdoor activity with a lot of fun and companionship as well as hard work. There were 15 foresters employed in Nethy Bridge when Jimmy MacLeod started work in 1952, women as well as men, and their tasks included gathering cones from 'granny' pines in the Abernethy Forest, extracting the seeds and sowing them in the nursery on Dell Road. They were then left to grow for two years, thinned to two inches apart, and left to grow for a further two years before they were ready for planting out in sites where the previous forests had been felled. Up to 1958, this was done with horses. Edie Robertson, whose father Peter McKerrell was one of these horsemen, remembers him getting up early to feed Rosie and Duncan and prepare them for the day's work ahead. The foresters were also involved in routine maintenance and until the 1970s, made all their own fence posts. Although in later years there were complaints about the introduction of non-native trees, 90% of the trees they planted were local Scots pine, although they also planted contorted pine, from Long Beach, California, for use as wind breaks and Norway spruce on wet ground as it was useful for soaking up water.

The last sawmill to be powered by water from the Nethy at the end of what is now Mill Lane, continued to run until 1965 by which time it had been in the McPherson family for 60 years. Mrs Celia Smart (nee McPherson), who was brought up there, remembers how they used to drop the sluice gates to close off the river, then lift them to let the water come down to fill the dam. A burn beside the house took the water back to the river and she remembers salmon and sea trout coming up this burn and her father and grandfather catching them in a net, knocking them out and putting them in the deep sink in the house. They would later be handed to the postman or other family friends.

On the Dell Road side of the Black Bridge, where there is now a house called Fearne Cottage, Joe Lobban ran a busy carpentry business. Joe, a fount of much local knowledge, lived nearby in the house called Alderbank, beside the Nethy, where his home-built, stone air raid shelter can still be seen. For many years the shelter was padlocked shut, appealing to the imaginations of many Nethy children who speculated on what might be inside. To their disappointment however, it was found to be empty. The carpentry business was later taken over by Robin McGillivray and then Douglas Crozier who continued to run it throughout the 1960s, providing training and work for many young men. Douglas Crozier was also for a time the village undertaker as well as a Sunday School teacher.

The Hydro-Electric schemes were promoted by the Government throughout the North and West of Scotland with a view to providing cheap electricity which, it was hoped, would encourage industry into the remoter areas. The nearest scheme to Nethy Bridge was probably Loch Laggan, south-west of Newtonmore, but men throughout the Highlands went to wherever the work was. In the case of Nethy men, this was mainly at the stage when pylons were being erected to transport the new power across the country: working 'on the pylons' was a common job description during the 1950s and 1960s. As this came to an end, many local men travelled to England to find work with one group moving to Basingstoke, where they were involved in building the new prefabricated houses. Some stayed away but many returned, sometimes bringing southern wives with them.

At the school, headmaster John Mathieson was succeeded by John MacLeod who went on to become Depute Director of Education for Inverness-shire. Both were native Gaelic speakers from the West of Scotland, as was their predecessor Kenneth Fraser, so there was much enthusiasm for Gaelic singing, with choirs regularly attending local and national mods. John Mathieson's wife Violet also trained a popular and successful adult Gaelic choir.

The school at this point consisted of three stone buildings. Facing the road was the primary building with three classrooms and an entrance and set of toilets at either end, one for the girls and one for boys. The middle building provided the junior secondary classrooms and the staff room. At the back was the canteen which also served as a gymnasium when PT or 'drill' was taught inside. More often, drill was outside, on the football pitch behind the canteen. As school numbers expanded and four primary teachers were required instead of three, a hut was built in the playground for the extra class. Closure of the primaries at Brig o' Broon, Tulloch and Dorback swelled the numbers in the primary, with these pupils and others from beyond a three-mile radius being transported by school cars, driven by such as Mrs Agnes Black, Laintachan and Dick George, Lynstock.

In the late 1960s, with James Stewart now headmaster, a new, large, concrete complex of buildings was erected as part of a country-wide school building programme. These were connected to the original front two buildings, with a gymnasium which also served as a theatre, plus purpose-built facilities for technical and domestic subjects. The old canteen building became a swimming-pool. Unfortunately, much of the new building became redundant just a few years later, when the introduction of comprehensive education closed down the junior secondary departments.

Throughout the 1950s and early 1960s there was still a variety of shops in the village. Willie MacKenzie's butcher shop behind the Drill Hall was taken over, soon after the war, by George Mustard who had been stationed in the Highlands with the Army during the war, married a local girl and chose to remain here. In the late 1950s he moved to smarter, larger premises – the former Cooper's store in Station Road which had been standing empty. Stewart's the baker's was in Nethy House until it closed in the 1960s and was taken over by the Hotel as staff accommodation. It is noticeable that, of all the buildings in the centre of Nethy Bridge, this one has changed least in outward appearance since it was built in the 1890s. On the corner of Station Road, the other side from the butcher's, Mrs Kliene sold all manner of fancy goods. She and her husband moved here in the 1950s, but he died soon afterwards, leaving her to run the shop on her own. She is remembered as a rather sophisticated woman, with a 'Morningside' Edinburgh accent, but she played a large part in the community. A Cup awarded annually by the WRI for their competitions is named after her. Next to Mrs Kliene's, (briefly) was a general store run by one of the Newfoundland foresters who stayed on after the war and next to that a newsagent, run by Eileen McPherson (wife of Tommy, who drove the Cooper's van).

Across the bridge, 'Donnie's' (MDC MacKenzie's grocery shop and Post Office) continued to thrive, with Hamish Marshall running the Post Office side of the business. Hamish, son of the Grantown forester and nephew of the Nethy forester, was more of an outdoors type, a keen fisherman and authority on the Cairngorms and their wildlife, so it was no great surprise when he left the Post Office to become a fishing ghillie on the Spey. His position was taken over by Sheila More, another stalwart of the community, involved in the drama group and the WRI and particularly remembered for playing the accordion to provide the music for village concerts. Donnie himself retired in the late 1960s and the shop was taken over by Dan and Anne Burns.

The Co-op continued until the mid-1960s in what is now Granite Cottage, while along the road at Duack Bridge, Maggie Methven still sold bakery goods, but had started to obtain her bread from Burnett's, delivered by vans, rather than freshly baked in the village. When her shop finally closed, it was taken over as a home by Gordon Mackintosh, coal merchant, who kept his coal supplies there or at the station. Gordon also drove the snow plough and gritting lorry during the winter months. Stocks of sand and grit were kept beside the road at the top of Balnagowan Brae, with a chute down to what is now Mill Lane to enable him to load it onto his lorries. The remains of this chute can still be seen today.

The village garage was bought in 1953 by Norman Smith whose family owned farms and garages around Alford, Aberdeenshire. Norman, who had recently left the Army and wanted to set up on his own, was said to have fallen in love with the area, but it was only a couple of years before he moved to Grantown, taking over the garage there as well as McKay's bus company. So the Nethy garage was sold again, this time to the Ross family who already owned the garage at Dulnain Bridge. Bob, who was the father of today's local funeral director John Ross, ran the Nethy garage while his brother Chad was in charge in Dulnain Bridge.

Up at the Causer, where the council houses now provided many new customers, McAndrew's 'wee shoppie' was taken over by Bob Harrold and then, in the 1960s, was replaced by a more solid, concrete structure, run by Mr Milne. The house 'Inveran' now stands on the site.

The Church still played a role in village life though successive ministries of the Rev. Ian McAllister, William Gardiner Scott and James Boyd. Most children attended Sunday School and there were two services on a Sunday, morning and evening. Since the evening service tended to have a smaller congregation, a heavy, deep red curtain would be drawn across the pews, halfway back, creating a cosy, intimate atmosphere. In the summer, the morning service alternated between the village church and the old Abernethy Church. To satisfy people in the outlying areas, the minister also held monthly services in Kincardine Church, attended by people from Tulloch, and in the Dorback School. The Rev. Ian McAllister had been minister since 1942 and seemed to be the steady, traditional type who changed very little about the church or the form of worship. A dignified individual, with a dry sense of humour, he enjoyed writing and left a legacy of poems which he had written about his time in Nethy Bridge. He also kept bees, though much of the work of looking after them was carried out by the 'beedle' or caretaker, whose other duties involved carrying the Bible to the pulpit at the beginning of the Sunday service. Mr McAllister used to relate how, on one of these occasions, the beedle walked solemnly down from the pulpit, then leaned towards the minister and whispered in his ear: "Your bees is a' deid!" Whether this was as a result of disease or just the cold weather is not known.

The Rev. William Gardiner Scott, who arrived in 1960, was a different prospect. A Glaswegian married to a Californian, with a Palestinian adopted daughter, he had previously preached in Jerusalem, from where he took the small, wooden cross which can still be seen behind the pulpit in the Nethy Bridge church – an unusual piece of ornamentation for what was still the very starkly decorated original Free Church. He also introduced a midnight carol service on Christmas Eve, which horrified some of the traditionalists by having candles in the Church. They saw this as smacking of Catholicism. Under his ministry, the Sunday School became Junior Church, while the 'kirk soiree' or AGM was revolutionised by the introduction of a barbecue tended by men of the Kirk Session – seen by some as a very undignified role. Maybe 1960s Nethy Bridge was not quite ready for his methods and after his departure in 1966, the Church reverted to the rather more traditionalist, more laid-back Rev. James Boyd. Under his ministry, Nethy Bridge combined with Cromdale, so that he had to hold Sunday morning services in both churches. At the same time, Kincardine became part of the Boat of Garten parish.

Tourists continued to come to the village, but times had changed and there were no longer all the wealthy families prepared to take a house 'for the season'. Often, the same families kept up their contact with the area with the younger generation indulging in the relatively new pursuit of camping, either with tents or caravans. Outdoor pursuits, such as walking and climbing in the Cairngorms, were particularly popular with tourists as well as locals.

Sporting tenants continued to visit year after year, such as the Naylor family to Forest Lodge and the Glendynes to Aultmore. They became part of village life during the late summer months of August and September, making donations to the local Games and Sheepdog Trials, but they were not keen to allow people to wander freely on their estates. The sporting estates, especially Dorback, also provided seasonal employment for students and older schoolchildren as beaters during the grouse-shooting season in August.

A new hotel was established when Heatherbrae Villa was taken over by Bill Philpott, one of the Newfoundlanders who had worked in the forests during the war – though in his case, not at Nethy Bridge. Bill married a Scottish girl, Mary Macdonald from Laggan, and they took over Heatherbrae as soon as it was de-requisitioned from its wartime Army use, opening it as an unlicensed guest house, which also served meals.

Mrs Fotheringham's ownership of the Nethy Bridge Hotel ended in the early 1950s, when it was sold to Hugh Fraser and then, soon afterwards, to the Aviemore Hotel Company, previous owners of the Station Hotel at Aviemore which had been destroyed by fire. She remained in the village, taking over the farm of Balliemore, the previous factor's house. The hotel was managed by Hugh Ross who, like his predecessors, became a member of the Strathspey Farmers' Club – proving that agriculture was still an integral part of the community.

The tourist season was still a short one, generally starting at Easter and ending in October. Throughout the long, cold winter months, hotels and guest houses were closed up and water turned off to prevent the horror of frozen pipes, while Nethy people reverted to a winter programme of whist drives, WRI meetings and their own company.

This was to change in 1961 with the completion of the ski road up Cairngorm and the formation of the Cairngorm Chairlift Company. It created a massive car park, a restaurant, a chairlift and several ski tows in the area which had previously been the preserve of ptarmigan, dotterel, shepherds, hill-walkers and a few hardy souls with Nordic cross-country skis. Now winter sports became a viable activity and brought a new generation of young, energetic tourists into the area, requiring to be accommodated, fed and entertained. Hotels and guest houses began to open for a winter season, from around New Year to Easter. After the sudden death of Hugh Ross, the Nethy Bridge Hotel employed a new managing director, Colin Sutton, who founded the Scottish Norwegian Ski School. The Heatherbrae Hotel acquired a license and was taken over by the Rileys, who took a particular interest in ski-ing. Their sons Martin and Duncan became the first Nethy Bridge youngsters to compete in competitions.

The rise of winter sports, coinciding with more spending power among the working classes, led to the next major shift in the economy and character of Strathspey: the Aviemore Centre.

Up to the mid-1960s, Aviemore was the place where you caught the sleeper train for London. Like the other villages around, it had a railway hotel, but little else to offer visitors. In previous centuries there was an inn, where the Winking Owl now stands, appreciated by travellers by stage coach or on horseback from the South. For Elizabeth Grant of Rothiemurchus, it was the place where she forded the Spey to reach her Highland home after a stay in London or Edinburgh.

All this changed in 1966 with the opening of the Aviemore Centre, conceived by Sir Hugh Fraser of Allander and designed by architect John Poulson. For many of the locals, the modern, concrete structures were viewed with horror, the multi-storey Strathspey Hotel being nick-named 'the sair thumb' because it stuck out like one.

For the young, however, it was a magical place which enabled us at last to join the 'swinging sixties'. The opening celebrations included a dance, with Radio 1 breakfast DJ Tony Blackburn and music by chart-topping band The Love Affair. There was a swimming-pool, an ice rink, a large modern cinema, shops and several bars. Coaches brought people from places such as the Moray Firth ports for the evening concerts and dances, while trains brought holidaymakers from the industrial belt.

It also provided much welcome employment, with jobs in the new hotels for Nethy women, while many strong young men, after their day's work on farms or forestry, were welcomed as security men or 'bouncers' from the evening into the small hours. On the down side, it could be seen as leading to the demise of local entertainment in places such as Nethy Bridge – to young people, local dances in the Community Centre lacked the glamour of 'the Centre'.

It could also be seen as the defining moment when Strathspey and Badenoch – rebranded as the Anglicised 'Spey Valley' (a name much hated by the locals) – became primarily a place for tourism and leisure and no longer a place where local people lived and worked in the traditional industries.

A very different type of development began in Nethy Bridge at around the same time. In 1965 Mr Norman Walker, the owner of Pitlochry Knitwear, bought the House of Abernethy, the original manse, which had previously been owned by a Mrs Ovens. Mr Walker was much involved with the Crusaders, a Christian youth organisation, which had previously taken groups of youngsters into the area to take part in outdoor activities, some to the Nethy Bridge station, and he bought the grand house with this in mind. Six years later in 1971, he was to donate it to a newly formed organisation, the Abernethy Trust, under which guise it grew into an influential outdoor centre with a Christian background, welcoming school groups and youth organisations from all over Scotland.

The other great change of the 1960s was that which affected the whole of rural Britain: in 1965, just over 100 years since the railways had opened up the Highlands of Scotland to the outside world, the small lines were pulled up, under the orders of Dr Beeching. Steam trains on these lines had by then been replaced by diesel, with a railbus known locally as 'the Sputnik' (in honour of the Space Race taking place at the time) taking passengers down Speyside to Craigellachie, where it was possible to change on to the main-line train to Aberdeen, returning later that day. After the Beeching cuts, the main line still stopped at Aviemore on its way to Inverness, disgorging hundreds of passengers to holiday in its centre or take the bus up Cairngorm to ski. The lines which passed through Nethy Bridge and Broomhill stations, to Craigellachie and Forres were closed to passengers, although freight trains continued to use the Speyside line for a few more years.

Now, holiday-makers were more likely to arrive by car and a new trend arrived: holiday cottages. In Nethy Bridge, where once the cottage was for the local family to move into in the summer, while wealthy guests rented the big house, now it was the cottage that they rented out. Farmers who did not already have a cottage on their land received grants to build one, as part of 'diversification.'

Gradually, too, new houses began to be built around the village – not by locals but by new people moving into the area from all corners of the British Isles. They were tucked into open spaces along Dell Road, Balnagowan Road and around the Causer. New, modern, pre-fabricated building methods were used and people marvelled at how quickly some of these houses sprang up.

Slowly but irrevocably, community life changed. Shops began to close as more people acquired cars and were able to drive farther afield to shop. The baker's at Duack-side closed, as did the one in Nethy House which became a hostel for seasonal staff at the hotel, then the Co-op, which reverted to a private house. At the Causer, the blacksmith closed in 1968, with the untimely death of the young, popular John MacDonald, son of Jim who had taken over between the wars. Since there were by now few horses to shoe, John had installed an electrical welding machine and specialised in beautiful wrought iron work.

Looking back on childhood years is always an exercise in nostalgia, but I do feel it was very special to grow up in Nethy Bridge in the early 1960s. The village was still small enough to know practically everyone –or at least, if I didn't know them, they certainly knew me! There seemed to be a large circle of elderly ladies, spinsters and widows, mostly living by themselves in the older houses of the village. They seemed to me to be very prim and proper, attended the Women's Guild and always wore hats, stuck with hat pins. We would never have dreamed of referring to them by their Christian names, so those with common surnames were identified by the names of their houses. Miss Grant Balnagowan lived, as her nickname suggests, in the house at the top of the brae. We used to visit her for afternoon tea as she was distantly related to us and my father always seemed slightly in awe of her as she had taught him in Primary School and had been very strict. I remember him telling me that he and his brothers always set out for school from Lettoch wearing boots but, as soon as they were out of sight of the house, they would take them off as they were much more comfortable without them and most of the other village children didn't wear them anyway. However, if Miss Grant saw them in bare feet they would be in awful trouble, as she would threaten to report them to their parents! Although she seemed stern, she had a great interest in everything that was going on in the world and was one of the first in the village to acquire a TV, which we were invited to come and watch with her. Miss Younger, several doors along in Grianach, was an incomer whose family had been among the original summer visitors. She was considered to be of a different social class – and these things were important at the time – but in later years she and Miss Grant became firm friends, getting together every Sunday evening to watch *Songs of Praise* on Miss Grant's TV. The Miss Christie sisters lived at Garlogie, opposite the football pitch. Their father had been Chief Constable of the Police in Greenock, though their grandfather came from a farm at Garlogie – hence the name of their house. May was very active and played the organ in church, but Daisy stayed at home because she was considered 'delicate'. The Miss Christies later moved to Nether Dell and Daisy lived well into her nineties, by which time she had become a grand old lady in Mount Barker nursing home. Miss Stewart Feorag lived on Duack side and supported anti-vivisection. Once a year, my friend and I went round the village for her, selling flags for charity, probably RSPCA. Mrs Jackson lived in Culvardie and taught in the Sunday School. She was an aunt of Gordon Jackson, then a very familiar star of stage and screen, who starred in British films such as *Geordie* and *The Prime of Miss Jean Brodie* and, later, in the TV shows *Upstairs Downstairs* and *The Professionals*.

There were local characters, too, such as Willie MacIntosh, otherwise known as 'the Little Ord', who worked for Miss Jessie Robertson on the farm of Balno. He is said to have driven all over Europe as a chauffeur in the early days of the motor car and he had a most impressive droopy moustache, but like so many Nethy residents, was a little too fond of the whisky. Once a month, when he was paid, he used to take his tractor down to the village pub, park it outside and drink until he was well and truly full. It is said that the village policeman Tom Johnston, on recognising the tractor, would remove the key, thus preventing the crime of drink driving – a real case of community policing! Another striking character was George McKenzie, who always wore a bow tie and looked very dapper. He was the son of A.G. McKenzie, former owner of the hotel, and had originally run the hotel garage, but by the 1960s had retired and was simply a 'presence', involved in various committees.

The big events of the year were the Nethy Games, held at that time in late August when the summer visitors were still around, but we children were already back at school after the holidays. The best part of the Games for us children was the 'Shows', run by the Spencer family, which would be at 'the Island' (beside the Nethy, opposite and down from the butcher's shop) for the week of the Games. The Spencer boys used to attend our school for that week and I was always amazed to see them transformed in the evening from schoolboys into businessmen, taking our money and giving out change with ease. Halloween was a tremendous event in which every child participated. There was the WRI party, with prizes for fancy dress and neap (turnip) lanterns (no pumpkins for us!) and then everyone went 'guising' round all the doors, with the onus on us to perform a song or poem – none of the unpleasant American 'trick or treating' of later days. At Christmas time the WRI organised another party, but Christmas Day celebrations were pretty much for children and not a general holiday, in fact the local shops were open and newspapers were available. New Year was something else, however, with all the traditions carefully observed and a round of visiting or 'ceilidhing' that went on well into January. On Hogmanay it was important to clean the house from top to bottom and finish off all tasks. I remember being told off by my Granny for starting some knitting on Hogmanay – she told me it would never be finished! Just before midnight, my Father went outside with his gun to fire two shots: one before the Bells, to shoot the Old Year out; the other after, to shoot the New Year in. We stood on the doorstep, in what always seemed to be clear frosty air, and listened to the shots from all the other farms around. Then the first footing started and it was very important that the first person to enter your house would be a dark-haired male, bringing peat or coal for the fire and something to eat or drink, to ensure that your wants would always be supplied for the coming year.

Summer or winter, we all spent much of the time outside. There were no proper playparks – you had to go to Grantown to find a swing – but there was always a place for football, skipping, marbles or a game of hide and seek and many of us enjoyed fishing for trout in the burns. If the sun was hot we could bathe in the pools of the Nethy and the Dorback and if there was frost and snow we made some spectacular slides – usually on roads or paths, which drove the grown-ups crazy! Outings were to attend football matches in the village, where Nethy still played in the Strathspey League, or to the cinema in Grantown, now the British Legion building.

These post-war years were certainly a period of growth and changes in Nethy Bridge, but it was an event at the end of the 1960s which was to lead to a fundamental change in the character of the place. In 1969, the Countess of Seafield died and her estate was split between her two children: the Earl of Seafield and Lady Pauline. The role of the Seafield estate and land ownership in the area were about to move into a new era.

Chapter 7

1970 – 2000 – Transformation and Conservation

For older inhabitants of Nethy Bridge, it is easy to see the years after the close of the railway lines and the rise of Aviemore as all downhill, with the gradual loss of shops, garage, police station and secondary school. There has been a huge shift in population, too, with people moving in from all over the United Kingdom, Europe and further afield so that the local accent is almost a rarity – a far cry from the days when I was laughed at for 'talking English' because my Mother had moved here from south of the Border soon after the War. Pronunciations have also changed, with the Causer (traditionally pronounced Cowser) now sounding the way it spells. Cairngorm is regularly being stressed on the first syllable rather than the second while Revack and Dulnain work the other way round, and Brig o' Broon has become Anglicised to Bridge of Brown! This last one is nonsense, since the 'Broon' at the end of the word comes from the Gaelic 'Bruthainn', meaning sultry, oppressive heat and has nothing to do with the colour brown. Dr Forsyth spells it 'Bridge of Bruin' which would be a good way to avoid the confusion.

We would do well to remember that the village has always been in a state of flux and very few of us can go back more than a generation or two without finding some 'incomer' on at least one side of the family. It is just that change seems to have accelerated so fast, as with everything else, since the middle of last century. As for the pronunciations, they are hard to pin down as they have gradually diverged from the original Gaelic and even Gaelic scholars are in constant disagreement, since the Strathspey version was apparently quite different from that spoken in the West of Scotland. A little basic understanding might help to avoid aggravation , such as stressing the most important part of the word, 'Gorm' (meaning 'blue') rather than 'Cairn' meaning 'mountain'), and knowing that "ack" at the end of words like "Revack" and "Bynack" is just like "y" at the end of an English word, so it makes no sense to stress it.

One reason for the transformation of the village was the break-up of the Seafield Estate after the death of the Countess of Seafield in 1969. The estate, which owned almost all the land in the area, was divided between her son, the 13th Earl of Seafield, and her daughter, Lady Pauline Illingworth. Lady Pauline inherited the Revack and Dorback estates, which included many of the farms around Nethy Bridge as well as the land on the Causer side of the River Nethy. She took these over with a great deal of enthusiasm, touring the farms with the estate factor, introducing herself to her tenant farmers and discussing her plans for the area. Unfortunately for her, the times did not favour large estates and she was to find that the burden of taxation forced her to sell off parcels of land, with first option going to the existing tenants. Thus some of the farmers were suddenly in a position to become owners of the land which had been tenanted by them and their ancestors – a huge and sometimes frightening step, but one which proved a boon for those able to take up the offer. Plots of land were also sold off to individuals and housing organisations and this led to an explosion of new houses in the area and, consequently, an influx of new inhabitants. Forestry plantations were sold to companies which took them on as an investment. In the 1990s, while married to her fourth husband, Lady Pauline transformed Revack Lodge near Grantown into a tourist attraction with a café, shop, woodland walks and an orchid nursery, but in 1999, having developed breast cancer, she sold off all her remaining land in the area. For the remainder of her life, she lived between homes on Tobago and in the south of England, dying in Dorset in February 2010.

The Revack Estate went to a property company which sold off individual parts, with first option going to the sitting tenants. Dorback, which consisted mainly of rougher hill grazing, was sold to a French businessman as a shooting estate, marking the final demise of an area that had once been populated by numerous small family farms and where sheep had grazed in the summer, tended by shepherds who knew every slope and hollow, every plant and bird. Now grouse and deer are bred for shooting parties, mainly from Continental Europe, while the new owners boast their 'green' credentials, claiming that they are rescuing the area from years of exploitation. They do provide some employment, for gamekeepers as well as people to look after the new lodge they have built and continue to employ young local people as beaters during the shooting months.

The land on the other side of the Nethy, including much of the Abernethy Forest, went to the Earl of Seafield, who continued to run the forestry operations initially, although the number of staff was gradually depleted as independent forestry companies began to undercut estate-owned operations. The nursery in Dell Road closed down in the 1980s and in 1993 the estate foresters were all laid off, marking the end of a way of life. Much of the land along the riverside and the forests between Dell Road and Tulloch have, however, remained in estate ownership.

From 1975, a new landowner appeared in the area – the Royal Society for the Protection of Birds (RSPB), which began to take over sections of the ancient Abernethy Forest and later the post-war plantations. Conservation of bird, animal and plant life was now all important, with forestry no longer seen as a money-making industry. The RSPB presence in the area had begun in 1958 when, after the return of the osprey to Loch Garten, they had undertaken the care of the area around the nest under a management contract with the Seafield Estate. In 1975 they bought over the area around Loch Garten, Loch Mallachie and a part of the Garten Wood, followed in 1979 by the Tulloch Moor. In 1983 they bought the rest of Garten Wood and then, in 1986, a large section of the Cairngorm Plateau, where the Lurg sheep used to roam, as well as Tore Hill behind Tulloch. In 1988 they bought the Forest Lodge estate from the Naylor family, transforming the lodge into their headquarters in the area, as well as a centre for eager volunteers, who came from all over the country and abroad to help with their work of conservation. Two years later, the purchase of North Abernethy tied everything together. Meanwhile Dell Wood, nearer the village, was taken over by Scottish Natural Heritage and this, combined with the now massive RSPB reserve, became the Abernethy National Nature Reserve.

Not surprisingly, this massive takeover did not find complete favour with the locals, who often felt that the area was being managed for the benefit of birds rather than people and that the traditional ways of life – farming, forestry and crofting – were being negated. Ross Watson of the RSPB points out, however, that RSPB did not make the rules. The areas were designated for special protection by British and European Government bodies and, as such, there was an obligation to protect such species as the iconic capercaillie. As landowners, moreover, the RSPB have been considerably more welcoming to walkers and mountain bikers than were the traditional shooting estates. There is no doubt that their presence in the area has encouraged the latest wave of visitors – wildlife tourism, with follow-on benefits to people providing accommodation or other services throughout the community.

In 2002, the RSPB added to their holdings the Sleamore and Craigmore forestry plantations on the other side of the Nethy, purchased from the

Revack Estate. These had been planted in the 1960s and the new owners immediately undertook the task of thinning out the trees to let in more light and create a better habitat for wildlife.

Farming, meanwhile, changed dramatically. New European breeds of cattle took over from the familiar black Aberdeen-Angus – Charolais, Simmental, Blondes d'Aquitaine – larger in frame and producing more lean meat, as demanded by health-conscious consumers. The old, granite, slate-roofed steadings, where cows used to be tied up in their stalls throughout the winter, went out of fashion. In came vast, concrete and corrugated iron structures where larger herds of cattle were left loose, with a big feeding area in the centre. Farmers became less weather-dependent, as they ceased growing oats and replaced hay with silage, which did not require to be dried out before storing. Most strikingly, the number of farms decreased as small units became no longer economically viable. The few remaining farmers now run several farms each, while traditional farmhouses have been bought up, often as holiday homes. Huge tractors and implements of all kinds mean that there is no longer work for farm labourers, even for seasonal tasks. A few hill sheep remain, but community sheep-shearings (or clippings, as we call them here) no longer take place, as there are not enough people with the skills to attend them. Farmers either clip their own sheep or engage contractors.

With the traditional industries dying out, a possibility of new employment for local people seemed to be raised when Justerini and Brooks proposed building a whisky distillery in an area of forest and bog between the Garlyne and Lettoch. This was to be used in the blended Scotch J&B Rare, a brand which, at the time, was almost all exported. The company sank a number of big, concrete wells, which can still be seen in the area, to test the water. Inhabitants were split between those who disliked the idea of desecrating the wilderness and those who saw it as a source of jobs. A public meeting was held, at which many angry voices were raised. In the end, however, an unexpected worldwide slump in whisky production forced the company to abandon the scheme.

So from the 1970s onwards, tourism was undoubtedly the main industry in Nethy Bridge, with people moving in from all over Britain (if not the world) to take part in offering accommodation: self-catering cottages, guest houses or bed and breakfasts.

All this did not occur without some friction and Elizabeth Fleming remembers a time in the 1970s when posters attached to lamp posts demanded 'English Go Home'. Things settled down eventually as natives and incomers learned to jog along together more-or-less satisfactorily.

Some new community facilities benefited locals as well as holidaymakers, an example being the recovery of the tennis courts behind the Community Centre. These had been created before World War II but had been allowed to fall into disrepair. In the 1970s a group of people got together to clear them of trees and weeds and also to raise money for their restoration. With the addition of grants from the Sports Council and local council two all-weather tarmac courts and changing rooms, were created, used by locals and tourists. There is an honesty box for donations.

Horse-riding also became possible when the hotel stables, at the back of the hotel gardens and behind the butcher's shop, were sold to Pat and Newby Taylor who set up an accredited riding school. Broomhill Court housing estate was later built on the site.

In the mid-1970s, a big change occurred in the life of the village with the closure of the junior secondary department of Abernethy School. Comprehensive education brought about the end of the 'qualifying' exam for 12-year-olds and that, combined with the raising of the school leaving age to 16, meant that all pupils proceeded to a secondary education with Ordinary or Higher-grade exams at the end of it. All secondary-age children now travelled by bus to Grantown – an event that, in the early days, caused some friction because of traditional rivalry between the two places. It also meant that large sections of the newly expanded school, including the purpose-built technical and domestic science departments, were now surplus to requirements. Some of this space was used by Highland Council as an outdoor centre for pupils from elsewhere while one of the rooms was used for a newly-formed Nethy Bridge playgroup. The swimming pool, originally the canteen, was pulled down.

Travelling into the area was made much easier by a large-scale upgrading of the A9, the main route north. For much of the 1970s, local men and lorries were among the workforce, which transformed the winding country road into something much straighter and faster, with some stretches of dual carriageway to allow overtaking. Journey time to Inverness was pretty much halved, so that a trip there became a common occurrence, rather than a full-scale expedition. It was also now possible to commute to work there, or to attend college daily.

As tourism became the most important industry, the Fleming family bought the empty, dilapidated Dell Lodge and converted it into a number of holiday cottages. They had strong connections with the village which was where they had met during World War II, John being the son of the then minister, also John Fleming. Elizabeth's family had moved here from the south of England to live in Grianach, the home of their relative Miss Younger.

Brian Patrick bought the unused Smithy and some land beside it on which he built two holiday homes before converting the Smithy itself into a third. He later bought a number of other cottages throughout the village, which he also used for holiday lets.

The Nethy Bridge Hotel, managed by Colin Sutton and later by his son Ewen, continued to attract visitors, although its clientele became less exclusive. The grand families who could afford to take rooms or suites in large Victorian hotels for a week or two at a time had become few and far between and people were more likely to stay for weekend breaks. Its public bar continued to be supported by locals, coming to be called 'Budgie's Bar' after Bill Budge, popular barman throughout the 1960s and 1970s.

The early 1980s saw the end of the Sutton connection when the hotel was sold to Chris Brotherston. The small house at the Balnagowan side of the hotel was sold on and later demolished when the road was widened – something which proved a boon to the users of public transport since buses could travel up to the Causer and pick up passengers there. The hotel was later resold to a company called Forth Wines, an offshoot of Scottish and Newcastle Breweries.

Nethy House, which had been used as staff accommodation, was taken over by Richard Eccles, who had come to the area as an Army ski instructor. With his wife Patricia, he began to run it as an Army Hostel then, on being made redundant from the Army in 1992, he moved permanently to Nethy Bridge. He used some of his redundancy money to upgrade the accommodation, renaming it Nethy Bunkhouse and making it more suitable for groups of civilian holiday-makers. Often young people from around the world could stay there more cheaply than in traditional hotels. Later, they were to increase the amount of accommodation by buying Nethy Bridge station from the Revack Estate.

The smaller Heatherbrae Hotel on Dell Road remained popular, under owners the Nicholsons, followed by the Scrimgeours. Its public bar was patronised by people from Lynstock, who could walk to it across the Black Bridge, as well as those who lived close to it on Dell Road. At one point in the 1980s it became a centre of national Press interest as it was frequented by landowner Lady Pauline, who had earned the tag of 'Lady Chatterley' after having affairs with at least one of her gamekeepers. She later took up with the Heatherbrae owner, Dave Nicholson, who left his wife and four children to become her fourth husband in 1989.

The Grey House temperance hotel, on the other hand, was sold to the BP oil company as a holiday retreat for their Aberdeen-based oil workers, then, in the 1990s it was sold on again to become a family home. Just along the road, a new hotel, the Mount View, opened in the late 1970s in the house that had been the Dunan. Its bar was also open to the public, but as a more sophisticated lounge bar.

Aultmore House moved out of the hands of the Glendyne family in the 1970s and became, for a while, a finishing school for girls from around the world, later a bed-and-breakfast establishment with some self-catering cottages.

Possibly the greatest success story of these years was Abernethy Trust, the Christian outdoor centre in the old Abernethy Manse, established in 1971 after being gifted to the Trust by Norman Walker. In the first year the property, consisting of 30 acres, was valued at £53,000 and took in 570 guests, accommodated in dormitories in the original house and looked after by one full-time and one part-time member of staff. The accommodation was improved and expanded throughout the decade, with the building of a new dining room and bedrooms and the introduction of a skiing course, which allowed the centre to operate all year round. From the beginning, the staff felt it was important to become involved with the community through the local church, to which the groups were taken every Sunday morning. Lorimer Gray, who came to the Trust as Warden in 1975, also became the church's session clerk and he and his young, enthusiastic staff took over the running of the Sunday School, renaming it the Sunday Club. Other youth organisations were set up for different age groups of local children and the involvement has continued up to today.

In the 1980s, a swimming-pool, sports hall and squash court were built at the centre and these too were available to local people, when not in use by the thousands of youngsters who were now coming from schools and organisations all over Scotland. Other buildings in other parts of the country were also gifted to the Trust, namely on Arran, Ardeonaig on Loch Tay, Ardgour on Loch Linnhe and Barcaple in Dumfries and Galloway – all operating under the umbrella name of the Abernethy Trust. The Arran centre was later closed, with the proceeds going to support the others. In some ways, the Abernethy Trust operates almost as a separate village, but there are thousands of people all around the country who, on hearing the name Nethy Bridge, immediately equate it with the centre where they have enjoyed a special holiday or been introduced to a new sport. Some local people have also found employment there, but the majority of staff are young folk from other parts who come here for their 'gap year', sometimes staying much longer. One of their proud boasts is that there have been 103 weddings of people who met while working at Abernethy Trust.

A different type of business, well in keeping with the area, was set up in 1976 by Harry Jamieson, who had come to the area as an instructor with Colin Sutton's Norwegian Ski School. Harry moved into the former mill at Craigmore, where he set up Craigmore Rods, making hand-crafted fishing rods. Originally from Callendar in the Trossachs, he had trained with a company called Trossachs Rods and when that came up for sale, he bought it. Then, since the name didn't exactly suit the area, he renamed it Clan Rods. Ghillies on the salmon rivers of Scotland recommended his rods to their clients and they were sold to some well-known angling enthusiasts. Greg Norman, Nick Faldo, Billy Connolly, the Duke of Marlborough and even the Duke and Duchess of Rothesay (Charles and Camilla) are numbered among his clients. They are also sold abroad to countries such as Norway and Japan – the latter being an important customer since the Japanese discovered the joy of salmon fishing.

Another local craftsman Mr Teneroni, previously a chef in the hotel, took over the shop owned by Mrs Kliene, in Station Road, right beside the bridge, where he created pottery painted with attractive pictures of local wildlife, a popular gift for Nethy residents as well as visitors. This shop closed, however, in the 1980s. There was also briefly a coffee shop, run by Mrs Phelan, in Granite Cottage, the former Co-op building.

Another coffee shop, with the unlikely name of Pollyannas, opened in the previous Garlogie, the house next door to the former Police Station. Coffee shops never seem to have survived long in Nethy Bridge. This one lasted only a few years before becoming a craft shop, initially Oriental Crafts, later Scottish Crafts, then yet another self-catering cottage and finally, in 2005, the bed-and-breakfast now called Tigh na Fraoch.

There were more changes after Nethy Bridge acquired a new minister in 1980, the Rev. James MacEwen, who came here from the Stockethill parish in Aberdeen, though he had previously preached in a socially deprived area of Glasgow. As the church had recently sold off the manse in the combined parish of Cromdale there was money available which the Kirk Session decided to spend on improving living conditions for the new minister and his young family. The manse's wooden porch, which had rendered it impossible to keep warm, was removed and the rooms reorganised to create a more fuel-efficient home. At this time, the minister was still holding a traditional monthly service in the Dorback School and involved in the regular Dorback community picnic, but this came to an end when the school was sold off by the education authority and became a private home. During the Rev. MacEwan's tenure, a new hall was built beside the village church with funds raised mainly in the community. This replaced the old hall, round the back of the manse, which had originally been converted from the minister's stables, and it soon became a hub at which various organisations could meet. In place of the traditional annual Church sale of work, held in August to attract summer visitors, an annual charity shop was established, held for a week in the spring in the Church and Church hall. Enormous quantities of books, bric a brac, clothes, fabric and furniture changed hands and hundreds of thousands of pounds were raised for charities all over the world.

The Nethy Bridge Tourist Association (NBTA) was founded in 1984, apparently as a reaction to a suggestion to hold a pop concert on the football field. Some people felt it would not be in keeping with the character of Nethy Bridge and the type of family-based tourists they wished to attract. Instead, they decided to organise 'traditional' ceilidhs or Scots Nights – one in February and three in the summer, with pipers, dancers and music. A tourist brochure about Nethy Bridge was developed by Jack Philp and, with the advance of new technology, a Nethy Bridge website was set up, with information about the area, designed for the community as well as to attract visitors to the area. Local newsagent Mrs Sheelagh George also produced a booklet on Walks around Nethy, a forerunner of Explore Abernethy's work some twenty years later.

One transformation that typified the years from 1980 onwards was the growth of housing estates. These already existed of course in the form of council estates, with post-war Lynstock and MacKenzie Crescent being extended in the 1970s by Craigmore Crescent and Bynack Place. The Thatcher era's selling off of council houses gave long-term council tenants the chance to become home-owners but, inevitably, it created a need for more affordable homes for local people. This role was partly taken on by the Albyn Housing Association which had been set up north of Inverness in 1973 to provide housing for workers at the Invergordon iron smelter. From the 1980s, it worked in partnership with Highland Council to provide affordable homes for rent and assisted ownership. Broomhill Court and Dorback Place were built with this in mind.

In the early 1990s, a 'unique and exciting development' was advertised by McLeod Building Ltd of Grantown. This was Dirdhu Court, a new type of development for Nethy Bridge, an estate of new homes, built in the traditional materials of stone and slate. Plots could be reserved for £20,000 and buyers could request their own designs. The site was below the crossroads, on the edge of the School Wood and had previously been a field belonging to the McAndrew croft at the Causer.

Dirdhu Court was not looked on favourably by all the locals, especially in the early years when most of the houses seemed to be holiday homes, since it became a dark, empty area throughout the winter months. Gradually the place took on a more lived-in appearance as more people chose to live there permanently. Within a few years, as trees grew up and gardens started to mature, it bedded into its surroundings so that, as with every other housing estate, there came a time when people could scarcely remember when it hadn't been there.

More estates were built, including Mill Lane leading up the riverside to where the old Balnagowan sawmill had been and Lynstock Park on the site of the World War 1 POW camp. Each one was viewed with initial horror and deemed to be pretty much the end of Nethy Bridge as we know it, yet residents grew used to them before very long.

There was also criticism when a new row of substantial houses was built opposite the playing field towards Duack Bridge, on land which had once been farmed by 'the Old Crofter', and also another row of houses at the foot of Lettoch Road. In both cases, the locals grumbled that they were being built on top of bogs – not realising that building methods had moved on and architects were now able to cope with these conditions. This was reflected by one of the new owners calling his house 'Swamp Castle' – a joke which, I am told, wears thin when people are trying to sell property nearby!

Nethy Bridge lost a small part of its individual identity in the late 1980s when the Northern Constabulary decided to close down the Police Station 'on economic grounds'. After the departure of the last local policeman, Jonathan Campbell, the Community Council tried to reverse the decision but were told that the police station needed renovating, at a cost of between £15,000 and £30,000, before a new policeman could be installed. This was not to be and the house was eventually sold off. From 1994 to 1995, it was used as a sports hire and ski school, before being converted into a bed and breakfast, renamed Aspen Lodge, and more recently into a self-catering cottage.

The village garage was another casualty of these years although the actual buildings still remain at the foot of Balnagowan Brae, behind the house called Bunnahabhain. For some time in the 1980s it still existed as a filling station run by John Stapely, who also sold Sunday papers after the closure of Sheelagh George's newsagents.

As the population of Nethy Bridge tended to become more elderly, another need was satisfied for a while by the creation of an Abbeyfield home in Badendossan on Dell Road. This large villa had experienced a chequered past since it was built in the late 19th century to let to summer visitors. There probably just weren't enough families rich enough to afford to take such a large house for the season, so it was soon sold by the original owners, moving through various hands before being bought in the 1960s by shop-keeper and councillor MDC McKenzie and renamed Blairmore. In the 1970s it became a guest house, but it was taken over by the Abbeyfield Association in 1983 and converted into a sheltered housing complex, run by an enthusiastic committee headed by the Rev. Jim MacEwan. To help support it, fundraising activities were organised, such as an annual walk through the Revoan Pass from Nethy Bridge to the Green Loch, with a picnic supplied by local ladies. Sadly, the home was forced to close in 2004 as the cost of necessary improvements proved prohibitive. Funds were retained, however, and later used to subsidise the houses at Birchfield Court, while Badendossan was sold back into private ownership.

Throughout this era, the shop and post office changed hands several times. In 1977, it was acquired from Dan and Anne Burns by Jimmy Millar and his locally-born wife Jessie, the grand-daughter of a former Nethy postman, Alexander Grant. They sold it on in 1981 to Ian and Mairead Noble, and it was later acquired by Jim and Marion Rogerson who converted it, in line with the times, from a traditional grocer's to a 'mini-market'. For a while it was owned by Gavin Addie, who was also to acquire the 'wee shoppie' at the Causer, then in the early 1990s, it came into the hands of Andy and Kate Young. Under their ownership, the building was re-designed, with the post office becoming an integral part of the shop and the entrance door moved to the opposite side. The stock was increased to include books, souvenirs and more varied foodstuffs to satisfy the ever more cosmopolitan tastes of both residents and visitors and they began to open on Sundays, selling Sunday papers. They ensured that their name would not be forgotten in the village when they built a bungalow behind the shop, currently occupied by Andy's mother Rose, and called it Tigh nan Og (house of the young – or Youngs).

The closure of the 'wee shoppie' at the Causer in 1997 was much lamented, particularly since such a large proportion of the inhabitants still lived there rather than in the village centre and there was even, at one point, a petition to keep it open. It had remained a popular shop and meeting place for those in the Causer and Lynstock area, under a series of owners.

These included Peter Savage from North Kessock, then Barbara Murray, who had worked there under both Mr Savage and his predecessor Mr Leslie, then briefly Gavin Addie, who also owned the village shop, followed by Vera Mathieson and finally Robbie Smith, son of a previous owner of the village garage. Sustaining two village stores proved impossible against the rise of the big supermarkets. First a shoppers' bus began to transport people to Inverness, then there was word of a Tesco opening in Aviemore – an event which did actually occur in the week that the Causer shop closed. According to Andy Young, the two events coinciding meant that there was no immediate difference in his volume of sales: what he gained from the Causer, he lost to Tesco!

The butcher's shop continued to thrive under the enthusiastic ownership of Michael, son of George Mustard, who also introduced new lines such as chorizo, for more adventurous shoppers, and a wide range of burgers and sausages to satisfy the barbecue craze.

Also in the early 1990s, the Nethy Bridge Hotel acquired a new general manager, Robert Wiles-Gill, when it was taken over by East Kilbride-based Strathmore Hotels, a chain of seven – two in Fort William and the others in Oban, Perth, Harrogate and Cumbria. The group's sister company, Strathmore Travel, organises coach tours in Scotland and the North of England. Naturally, the hotel continued to attract coach tours, but it was also host to some exotic visitors such as Prince Georg, who claimed to be a member of the Hapsburg dynasty, as well as the future Afghan president Hamid Karzai who, along with an entourage including Special Branch, took over the whole hotel. He is said to have 'really, really loved the hotel' and Nethy Bridge in general – so much so that after he became President, he wrote requesting a picture of the village to place on the wall of his Presidential palace. The old public bar at the back of the building, behind what had been the hotel garage, was closed down, with the new public bar and games room being created at the side of the hotel, previously a lounge bar. The ballroom, where local dances had been held, became the Revack suite, for use of hotel patrons only, while the games room, originally used by gentlemen residents, became the new lounge bar.

The village also acquired a new schoolmaster in 1993 in the person of Howard Edge. He took over from Ewan Ross who had been the first schoolmaster not to live in the school house and whose wife Mary was an enthusiastic president of the WRI.

Howard inherited a large school building, much of which was standing empty. The technical room, complete with woodwork benches and forge, had been left unused for 20 years so, with funding available from the Education Department, he was able to turn it into what he claims is one of the largest infant classrooms in the country! Empty classrooms in the original part of the school were also turned into a library, art room and resource room.

The advent of the National Lottery and its attendant grants was also good news for Nethy Bridge. Lottery money was used to upgrade the Community Centre, turning it from a rather dingy hall into a bright venue which people were happy to hire for parties and ceilidhs. The tennis courts were also upgraded, partly with the help of money left in her will by former Nethy resident and Grantown schoolteacher Jessie Fraser.

A new and significant development occurred in the late 1990s with the creation of the Nethy Bridge Interpretive Project, later to become known as Explore Abernethy. Perhaps with the fear that much of old Nethy Bridge was being lost and forgotten, this project aimed to 'record and interpret the cultural heritage of the Nethy Bridge area'. The first phase, in 1997-98, was to create a network of way-marked paths, using walking tracks that had been known to generations of Nethy people but possibly fallen out of use. For the second phase, in 1998-99, the Explore Abernethy Room was set up in the Community Centre as a place where residents and visitors could find out about their heritage, both historical and environmental. This was not without controversy, since it meant losing the sports room with its snooker table, the latter being removed to the Nethy Bridge Hotel, on an indefinite loan.

The year 1998 welcomed two new pairs of hoteliers who were to make a big impact on the village. Jan and Mo Tomasik took over the Heatherbrae Hotel, which became very much a community pub hosting such events as the Senior Citizens' ceilidh and running an annual pool competition, quizzes and lucky numbers competitions to raise money for local organisations. It also became a pleasant place for family meals – in the cosy public bar beside a roaring fire or in the smart conservatory area. It was seen as a great loss to the village when, nine years later, the hotel closed down, having previously been sold by Jan and Mo, who had retired to Perthshire. There was much talk of a petition to keep the Heatherbrae open but in the end economics prevailed and it reverted to its original role, as a private house.

Meanwhile, Kevin and Caryl Shaw took over the Mount View, which they used as a base for Heatherlea, their wildlife-watching holidays which they had previously been running from a smaller guest house in Boat of Garten. As well as organising day outings with local guides in this area, they also ran wildlife trips throughout the Highlands and Islands and abroad. Holiday-makers on a budget, who enjoyed being surrounded by wildlife, were also catered for from 1999 with the opening of the Lazy Duck Hostel, built by David Dean and his wife Valery (daughter of the Flemings of Dell Lodge) in the woods behind Lynstock, beside the old, traditional cottage of Badanfhuarain.

In 1995, Bunkhouse owner Richard Eccles set up a Trust to buy the ruin of Castle Roy from the Revack Estate. Lady Pauline was herself one of the Trust members as was the local councillor and the chairman of the Community Council. Richard's aim was to turn Castle Roy into a site which people could visit, but it was to be another 17 years before any real progress was made.

There were signs of development in another direction when Nethy Bridge Pottery was established in 1998, in a converted steading at Culreach on the Grantown road. Passers-by could stop and watch as potter Rob Lawson made his distinctive pots, plates, bowls and ornaments in swirly shades of blue, green and purple. This may be seen as the forerunner of a developing trend of people moving into old properties to set up small-scale creative enterprises.

The second half of the 20th century had brought about a vastly transformed Nethy Bridge, which had lost several shops, its garage, police station, secondary school and much of its traditional industry, and gained a very disparate population as well as a variety of new housing estates. With tourism by far the biggest industry and conservation an over-riding preoccupation, it remained to be seen if the village could retain its identity and sense of community.

Chapter 8

The New Millennium: Nethy Bridge Today – and Tomorrow?

At the start of the new Millennium Nethy Bridge seems to have hit the ground running. Perhaps it was because the new housing developments had brought new people into the area, but there seems to have been a burst of fresh ideas as on so many occasions in the past. Explore Abernethy really got into its stride in the year 2000, when it began to employ a seasonal ranger to look after the centre and the network of paths. This has included laying on guided walks and events, as well as much involvement with the local primary school, helping them with projects which are often working towards their John Muir awards. By 2010 the post had been made permanent, although this status remains dependent on funding from year to year.

In September 2003, Nethy Bridge became a part of the Cairngorms National Park, bringing in yet another shoal of experts to remind us, in case we had forgotten, what a beautiful part of the world we inhabit. They have four stated aims: "to conserve and enhance the natural and cultural heritage of the area; to promote sustainable uses of natural resources of the area; to promote understanding and enjoyment (including enjoyment in the form of recreation) of the special qualities of the area by the public, and to promote sustainable economic and social development of the area's resources." Inevitably, this has promoted much debate, mainly as the park strives to achieve the balance between conservation and employment – or wildlife and people. Practically, it means that any planning application has to be approved by the Park as well as the usual authorities, which should ensure that all new building is in keeping with the surroundings. It has also meant that grants are available for fresh initiatives within the park, as long as they comply with its aims, and there have been no shortage of candidates within the village.

Of course all is not sweetness and light. As with any other small community, there are perpetual grumbles between different organisations and, specifically, between 'locals' and 'incomers' – though often the lines are blurred between the two. Just how long do you have to be in the community to be termed a 'local'? Partly with this in mind, the village founded its newsletter, *The Nethy,* in 2005 with the stated aim of 'Helping to Bring the Village Together'. Edited by farmer, businessman and entrepreneur John Kirk, it aims to report all that is going on locally.

As the decade progressed, there was a strong desire by many Nethy Bridge residents to embrace alternative technology, making use of such natural assets as sun, wind and timber. Solar energy panels appeared on the roofs of traditional and newly-built houses, wood-burning stoves were installed in numerous homes and, more controversially, a scheme was suggested to bring wind power from the hills above Corriechullie (on the Tomintoul road) to serve the village. The latter was initiated by the Community Council, who then formed The Nethy Bridge Community Development Company, specifically so that it could own assets on behalf of the community. The plan was to build a small group of wind turbines which would generate enough electricity to make the village self-sufficient, as well as selling some to the National Grid. Inevitably, the scheme has met much opposition, having to run the gamut of planning control by the National Park as well as the council and, of course, local opinion. At the beginning of 2012, permission had been granted to erect an anemometer on the site, which would measure the speed of the wind over a year to decide whether or not the scheme would be viable, but permission to erect the actual turbine was still a long way away.

The loss of the Heatherbrae Hotel in 2007 was seen as a blow to the community, as was the end of Sunday services in the old Abernethy Church in 2009. The future of this church had been in doubt for many years, since it was really not feasible to maintain two churches for a constantly dwindling congregation. Up to World War II, services were held there every second week throughout the year, but later they came to be held in summer only. Upgrading the old church to satisfy modern requirements was always going to be a problem since it stands in the middle of the graveyard, so that it is difficult to bring in services such as water and sewerage. The Dell Road church, on the other hand, was more central to the community and easier to adapt. When the Church of Scotland finally made the decision to sell the old church, there was much concern about its future, since the problems that made it hard to modernise also made it unsuitable for conversion – especially after it had achieved listed status in 1971. Rather than allow it to fall into disrepair, some residents formed a Trust, the Abernethy Old Kirk Association (AOKA), which succeeded in buying the church for the community in 2011. It is now a private company limited by guarantee and a registered charity. Weddings and funerals are held there, as well as events such as photographic exhibitions, occasional concerts and talks and a regular teddy bear festival. Recent lottery grants have enabled an interpretation project, the purchase of various display boards and equipment and, pending planning permission, the installation of a standpipe in the churchyard.

There was a coming together of different organisations within the village in 2010 to celebrate a major aspect of its heritage – the bicentenary of the Telford designed bridge around which Nethy Bridge took shape all those years ago and which has remained a focal point. This was the brainchild of Community Council chairman Sandy McCook, whose ancestors were involved in the bridge's construction and whose father Alistair is a previous local councillor. An interpretive board was erected, relating the history of the bridge's construction; the Chief of Clan Grant, Lord Strathspey, opened the proceedings a golfing 'Texas Scramble' was held, involving both serious golfers and less serious Nethy celebrities, and the ladies of the WRI provided tea and refreshments. Nethy Bridge went all out to celebrate its past.

Another anniversary was marked in 2011 – 100 years since the village hall had been handed over to the community, under the charge of a group of trustees which included the minister, the schoolmaster and the local councillor. With this arrangement coming to an end, a new committee was set up to manage the Community Centre. The same organisation has also set up a Community Woodland Project, which has taken over a section of the wood behind the Games field, gifted by the Seafield Estate. This is to be cleared of non-native trees, which have grown so thickly as to make the area almost impenetrable, in order to provide a pleasant area where people can walk, as well as a raised viewing area for the Highland Games.

Later in 2011, a change occurred which marked the end of one particular 60-year project. The giant pylons which had been erected in the 1950s to transport hydro-electricity across the country were dismantled and removed, piece by piece, by skilfully-manoeuvred helicopters. Although these monsters can scarcely have been considered things of beauty when they were first erected, and although at various times they were accused of such evils as causing cancers and depression, we had grown used to them and their going caused some pangs of nostalgia. As soon as they had gone and open vistas stretched for miles in every direction, it was hard to remember that they were ever there.

A more accidental loss was Rab McGinlay's sawmill at Forest Lodge, the last such enterprise in Nethy Bridge, destroyed by a disastrous fire which also took Rab's residential caravan and narrowly avoided spreading to the edge of the forest itself.

On a more positive note, Castle Roy, the long-term project of Richard Eccles and the Trust set up in 1995, finally got off the ground in 2012 with a £34,000 grant from Historic Scotland which is enabling the tower to be shored up. It is hoped to raise a further £175,000, with more help from Historic Scotland, as well as Scottish National Heritage and possibly the Lottery. There is also a scheme to sell off individual square yards of the castle to people abroad with nostalgic longings for 'the old country'. To this end the chiefs of Clan Grant and Cumming have been approached to spread the word. The eventual plan is to create a free visitor attraction with interpretive boards, pictures of what the castle used to look like, wheelchair access and, if possible, a flattened area inside the walls where concerts and other celebrations could be held. The area of land beside the road, bought from the council for £1, is being used as a builders' yard while the work is in progress and later will become a car park for the attraction.

Two new, and very different, housing estates have also appeared in the last couple of years. Birchfield Court, the latest Albyn Homes development, right in the centre of the village, consists of 13 homes, nine to rent and four to buy under the assisted ownership scheme. They were built with the help of a donation from the Abbeyfield organisation – money which had been retained after the sale of Badendossan – and a Housing Association grant. The homes are geared specifically towards the over-55s or those with a disability, and are super insulated and heated by air source heat pumps. They are designed in a courtyard layout, with a low stone wall in front, to give them a sense of community. The other is a Wellburn Homes development, Braes of Balnagowan, which is still looking rather stark and out of place in 2012, but may well bed in over time as all the other estates have done.

Jane Macaulay

One of the most frustrating things about the Rev. Forsyth's vast, informative work, *In the Shadow of Cairngorm*, which he wrote just over a century ago, is that he gave us little information about the world of his own day – assuming perhaps that the readers knew all about that, so it didn't need to be written down. Another century on, I wonder what people would make of the Nethy Bridge of today?

I would like to think that they would see it as a thriving, lively, friendly place where community spirit still holds sway, with neighbours keeping an eye on each other, people greeting each other as they walk past and a whole variety of organisations and activities for those who want to be sociable. Those who simply seek peace and quiet and beauty can find that, too.

This is still a breathtakingly beautiful area which has not been spoiled by insensitive development or mass tourism. Great sweeps of forest still encircle the village, bird feeders commonly attract red squirrels and woodpeckers and the occasional crested tit, alongside the more common garden birds. Well kept walking tracks, many of them accessible for disabled people, can lead us beside the sparkling, tumbling waters of the River Nethy, where we may stop to watch a dipper bobbing and diving, along forest tracks or across heather moors, with splendid views of the towering Cairngorms.

The two remaining shops, butcher's and grocer's, seem to be flourishing, with the butcher's supplying many of the hotels, guest houses and restaurants throughout the area, while the grocer's also houses a busy post office, still a hub of community life. Cars line up outside it on Sunday mornings, when people come to collect their Sunday papers; on Monday evenings when the mobile chip shop is parked outside, and on Thursday afternoons when the local paper, '*The Strathy*', comes out. Each of these occasions is a chance for locals to get together and chat. An early morning milk delivery three days a week supplies people throughout the village, while a fish van from Portsoy goes from door to door on a Wednesday as the old grocery and bakery vans used to do. A more recent development is the proliferation of Tesco and Asda delivery vans, as well as courier vans delivering goods ordered over the Internet. Although some see these as a threat to local businesses, they do make life much easier for people living in far flung parts and reduce the amount of fuel used in car journeys to and from the shops.

Buses every hour or two take people from the village and Causer bus stops to Grantown or Aviemore. Although the handful of people who use them grumble constantly when they are delayed, it is possible with a little patience and flexibility to use them to travel effectively throughout the area. In fact, the bus company, Stagecoach, held a recent public consultation which resulted in changing the times to fit in with trains at Aviemore and in the launch of a Sunday service, albeit limited. For the elderly or those with mobility problems, there is a very effective community car scheme staffed by volunteers.

The Nethy Bridge Hotel is still busy, attracting people from around the world, some on coach trips, some on weekend breaks. It also hosts various events such as a Rolls Royce owners' weekend in May, now in its 14th year. When all these magnificent vehicles line up in front of the hotel and in the field opposite, it takes us back to past days of opulence. Another weekend hosts MGs, while there are also get-togethers of motorbike and antique lorry clubs. The hotel also has a lounge bar, a public bar and a games room with a pool table and two snooker tables. The Mount View still runs its wildlife holidays and it serves popular evening meals, but there is a noted lack of a community pub or even a coffee house – a cosy space where we could get together and maybe take our visitors. The Community Centre has tried to compensate by holding coffee mornings, the 'Nethcafe', now and again on a Saturday, as well as a 'chippy night' on Mondays, when people can take advantage of the presence of the fish and chip van and take their meal inside to eat it and chat with others.

Groups of schoolchildren from all over Scotland make good use of the Abernethy Trust facilities in what was once the church manse, the minibuses with their distinctive logos being a familiar site around the village as they carry their passengers to take part in their outdoor activities or to attend the local church on Sunday mornings.

Explore Abernethy, the village's Interpretive Project, has proved a success, visited by people from other organisations, seeking ways to celebrate their own cultural heritage. The network of way-marked paths they have created around the village are well trodden by residents and visitors alike, with the most recent additions being 'Haemack's Road' – the retracing of the track once taken by cobbler and church handyman Hamish McKenzie from his home in Culvardie to his peat moss. Work is constantly going on to keep these in good order and to upgrade them, where possible, to all-abilities paths which can also be enjoyed by people with mobility problems. A mill lade, once used for the Duack sawmill, has been cleared for 100 yards in the wood behind Culvardie and a sluice built, along with an interpretive board explaining its history. The most recent plan, involving the local schoolchildren, is to create a wildflower meadow in a field beside the riverside path.

Meanwhile at Forest Lodge the RSPB has ambitious plans to double the size of the Abernethy Forest, bringing trees up to what they see as the natural tree-line on the side of the Cairngorms and returning the forest to its 'pre-Industrial Revolution' dimensions. This involves turning the planted woodland to 'woodland of natural character', while encouraging the existing Scots pine to spread outwards and planting areas of trees which are not regenerating. Trees are to be planted in clumps rather than in uniform rows and broad-leafed varieties such as birch, aspen, rowan and alder are to be encouraged rather than unmitigated pine, creating what they call a 'wooded landscape' rather than a forest. Double the amount of wooded landscape, apparently, should encourage double the amount of wildlife – there are already 4500 species of animal and plant life in the area and new varieties of lichen, spiders and beetles are being identified every year.

Some of the RSPB policies remain controversial, particularly their insistence on leaving dead wood lying and even knocking over some healthy trees – in some cases causing alarm by using explosives in the process. So where eager locals would once swarm over the ground picking up 'crackers' or fallen branches for their fires, fallen trees are now left as habitats for insects – a state of affairs which many people find untidy and unsightly. In an attempt to improve relations, the RSPB hold Family Fun Days every two years (on the years in between, the Fun Days are held at Insh Marshes) and these are genuinely popular, with more than half of the people attending being local rather than holidaymakers. A new initiative for 2012 was to involve the school's Parent Council, who organised the catering and retained the profits.

The village's permanent population is on the increase. In 2008 it was 610, though it is almost certainly larger now and it is said to go up to around 1500 in the summer months when all the holiday homes are occupied and tourists in residence. Certainly there is a greater proportion of over-60s than there would be in cities, since many people have chosen to retire here, some of them natives who have returned to the village after a lifetime of living and working elsewhere. At the same time, there is a respectable number of younger families with children who attend playgroup, nursery and primary school here and secondary in Grantown. Until recently a youth club operated in the Community Centre but this came to an end because of a perennial problem: not enough people with time to run it. There are the usual complaints that there is nothing for teenagers to do, but there do seem to be quite a few sporty youngsters who are happily occupied with golf in the summer and winter sports whenever weather conditions allow. The new Craig McLean Sports Centre in Grantown is popular with all ages and through this an 'Active School Co-ordinator' organises after-school activities in Nethy Bridge, currently a Fit Kids club, basketball, football training and the ubiquitous zumba. Staff from the Abernethy Trust also run clubs for youngsters and teenagers in the church hall.

The school itself had a healthy roll of 59, with 15 in the nursery, in the 2011-2012 session and it employs three full-time teachers as well as headmaster Howard Edge, who is also responsible for Boat of Garten Primary. The numbers are down from recent years when an eight-year 'bulge', brought about by new, affordable homes in the village, allowed the school to have four teachers. A record class of 20 primary 7s left for Grantown in June 2011. The pupils are a mix of Scottish and English with just a handful of other nationalities, namely Polish, Czech, Canadian and South African. The headmaster says the biggest change he has noticed in 19 years at the school has been the drop in the number of pupils from farms. Most of the parents, he says, are involved in tourism or work for the National Park, in Grantown, Aviemore or Nethy Bridge itself.

As ever, many young people leave the area to attend college or university or to pursue a career, but this has become less necessary than 30 years ago. There are jobs to be had in construction, conservation or the tourist industry – though many of these are seasonal – and the possibility of commuting to Inverness. Some have even set up their own businesses, for example, arboriculture, steel erection and the various aspects of building and maintenance.

Older people, or those with more time on their hands, are catered for in the many activities that take place throughout the day and the evening. For the sports minded there is indoor bowls in the winter and outdoor bowls in the summer, as well as the golf club which holds many competitions throughout the year and a particularly sociable seniors day on a Thursday. Snooker and pool can be played in the Nethy Bridge Hotel, tennis on the courts behind the Community Centre and the Abernethy Trust swimming-pool is available to locals when it is not required for groups.

There is a weekly lunch club, a health walk, a knitting and sewing group, a country dance group, regular whist drives and a gun club, with most activities offering the chance for a cup of tea and a chat. The local branch of the SWRI has a membership of around 40.

The annual calendar is a full one, too. As well as the Church-organised week-long, hugely popular charity sale in March, there is a plant sale in May and, for the past two years, the Nethy Bridge Tourist Association has organised a Spring Gathering, showcasing all the different organisations, with cakes for sale, refreshments on hand and races for the children. In July there is the Open Gardens, when we can satisfy our curiosity about other people's growing skills and, once again, enjoy a cup of tea and a cake. On the second Saturday in August, the grand event of the year, the Nethy Bridge Highland Games are held which have been going since 1880 (with a break during and between the World Wars). Its reputation is going from strength to strength, attracting visitors from all over the world and competitors of a very high calibre in events such as Highland dancing, piping, tossing the caber and other traditional heavy events, races for both children and adults and the heart-stirring, spectacular Massed Pipe Bands. Since the 1990s, the event has also comprised the Clan Grant Gathering and in 2010 there was even a Cherokee chief from the US, whose tribe was affiliated to the Grants. The organisation is an example of village co-operation at its best. Although the Games committee may include the same people as are found on various other committees in the village, there is a willing band of helpers without whom it would be impossible to stage. Their only remuneration is an invitation to a cheese and wine party in the autumn. At Christmas time the village is decorated with lights, organised by a Festive Lights Committee which gathers funds throughout the year and adds new decoration whenever finances permit. The year is seen out, on Hogmanay, with a torch-lit procession led by a piper from Lynstock to the Community Centre, with stovies in the Hall, organised by the Mothers and Toddlers' group.

So what of the future?

One dramatic change occurred in autumn, 2012, with the retirement of the very popular minister, the Rev Jim MacEwan, who has played a significant role in the community for the past 31 years. With several other local ministers retiring around the same time, there is to be a reorganisation of parishes. Abernethy will be separated from Cromdale, which will now be linked with Grantown, and will be combined instead with Boat of Garten,

Duthil and our old partner, Kincardine. It remains to be seen what effect this will have on the community. It is proposed that the new minister will be located in Boat of Garten, since this is more central, so the Nethy Manse will no longer be occupied by the minister.

Other matters, such as the wind turbine plan, remain in the pipeline. Neil Sutherland, who is chairman of Explore Abernethy and of the village development company, believes that the scheme could be of tremendous advantage to the community. By selling back power to the National Grid, it could generate hundreds of thousands of pounds which could then be used to create opportunities for young people as well as care provision for the elderly. It is, he believes, all about one of the National Park's stated aims of having 'active communities'.

The most recent house-building plan is for the School Woods – the area of woodland between the school and the village and behind the school as far as Torniscar, which has always been a popular place to wander. After lengthy negotiations, the developers, Tulloch Homes, have agreed to scale down their original extensive plans and to build on five hectares only, while donating the remaining 75 hectares to the village, to be kept as community woodland. This can be seen as either another tremendous opportunity for the community to shape its own destiny or as yet another bone of contention between developers and conservationists.

Not surprisingly, opinions about Nethy Bridge past, present and future are as varied as the inhabitants, with just a few points winning general agreement. There is general praise for our two remaining shops – Andy Young's general store and post office and Michael Mustard's butcher's shop – which are seen as among the best in the area, catering admirably for both inhabitants and tourists. There is universal agreement that we lack a community pub, coffee shop or eating place which could cater for both locals and for those staying at the village's many bed-and-breakfast or hostel establishments. Perhaps someone will appear within the next few years to fill such a glaring gap in the market. The Abernethy Games, too, wins plaudits as 'one of the best small Games in the country' and as an example of the village working together in harmony for a shared aim. Secretary Neil Sutherland cites the particular example of Roy Calder, a local man from a traditional local family, who rarely attends a committee meeting but turns up every year to mark out the field before the event. There is also the well maintained, well used Community Centre and well drained playing field.

Most people praise the strong community spirit. Neil Sutherland describes the village as 'a very fortunate place. As a community it seems to get on and do things and do things quite well – partly because of the situation and partly because of the kind of people who come and live here'. In a similar vein, Sandy McCook believes we are fortunate because 'so many people have come in and become involved' and he sees it as a go-head community which realises that 'we can't stand still but have to manage our progress carefully'.

There is also general opinion that it is a friendly place, but opinions are divided over just how well 'locals' and 'incomers' co-exist. Many people who have lived in other small communities believe that ours is more integrated than most, while others see no divisions at all. Richard Eccles, on the other hand, sees it as a community divided in three: 'indigenous families, long-term incomers and new incomers in the housing estates' and believes it is 'very difficult to get people to pull together'.

Locally born farmer and former Councillor Stuart Black points out that without the 'incomers' the village would be a much poorer place, unable to sustain the shops or even the school. He believes that many of the new people who have come in have brought positive new ideas, helping to keep it a very vibrant place and he is gratified to see that so many of them have taken an interest in preserving the culture. On the downside, he is aware that house prices have been raised, making it difficult for local young people to afford their own homes. With so many new young families here, however, he points out that their children will be the 'locals of tomorrow'.

Another perceived division is between the RSPB operation and others in the community, with many people seeing the RSPB as putting birds and animals before people. Ross Watson feels that people don't give the organisation a chance, focussing on negative things, such as 'painting Forest Lodge the wrong colour', while ignoring the positive things they have done. He feels that it is because they are so totally open about everything they are doing that they lay themselves open to criticism, unlike the estate-owners in the past.

Another vexed question is the provision of housing. There is general agreement that it is very hard for our young people to get a foot on the housing ladder while people from further afield can afford to pay high prices for houses intended as holiday homes or investments. Without affordable homes, young people may choose to leave the village, which would undoubtedly be a tragedy for community life – but it is difficult to see how this can be remedied. At the moment there are rules which force house builders to create a proportion of affordable homes, for sale and for rent, but there is an objection that all these homes are clustered at one end of a housing estate, creating a kind of class division.

As for the future, Sandy McCook says he can't ever see Nethy Bridge stagnating as a community – it has certainly never done so in the past – and he just hopes it will continue to 'move forward gently, while remembering where it comes from and maintaining its true character.' Neil Sutherland hopes there won't be too many more holiday homes, as he has seen so many people coming in, spending a lot of money on a property and then hardly ever being there. His hopes for the future are to: 'keep it going, keep up the number of young people involved, maintain continuity and do things to the best standard that we can.'

Nethy Bridge is many things to many people, but it never has been and never will be a static community, stuck in time like Brigadoon. Great changes have brought the village to where it is now, from the scattered homes of hunter-gatherers, to small communities of crofters and cottars

The Story of Nethy Bridge

clearing a space to live and grow a few crops, to the farming and foresting communities working in harmony with the seasons. The advent of the railways and the tourists, sporting estates, winter sports and wildlife tourism; from the days of one all-encompassing landlord to private and community ownership. One thing is certain: we can't go back, but we can move forward without forgetting all the things that make up our heritage. Nethy Bridge has had an amazing history and there is every chance that it will have an amazing future.

·The story of Nethy Bridge is a continuing one.